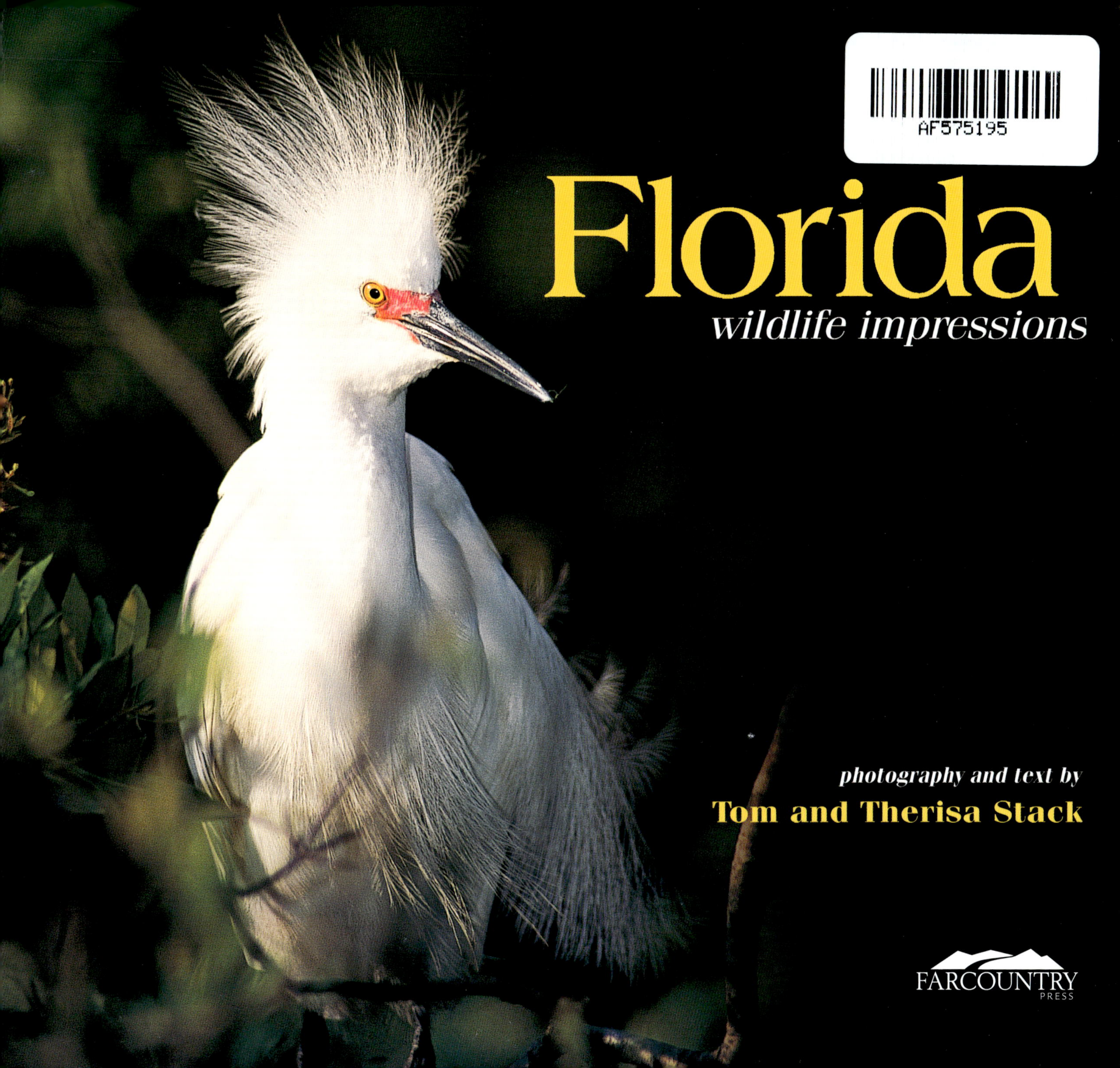

AF575195
Florida
wildlife impressions

photography and text by
Tom and Therisa Stack

FARCOUNTRY
PRESS

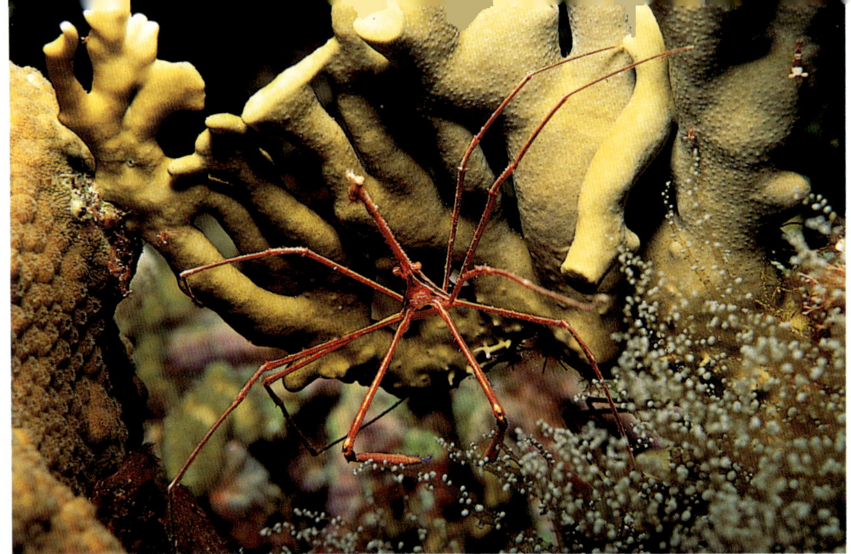

ABOVE: A two-inch arrow crab treads gingerly upon blade fire coral in the John Pennekamp Coral Reef State Park off Key Largo.

RIGHT: The rock beauty is an elusive and stunningly beautiful angelfish occasionally seen in the Florida Keys National Marine Sanctuary.

TITLE PAGE: Snowy egret in breeding plumage, St. Augustine, Florida.

FRONT COVER: A striking queen angelfish flaunts its colors in the John Pennekamp Coral Reef State Park off Key Largo.

BACK COVER: A great egret in breeding plumage wades amid red mangrove roots at the Florida Keys Wild Bird Center in Tavernier.

ISBN 1-56037-328-8

For more information about our books write Farcountry Press, P.O. Box 5630, Helena, MT 59604; call (800) 821-3874; or visit www.farcountrypress.com.

Created, produced, and designed in the United States.
Printed in China.

09 08 07 06 05 1 2 3 4 5

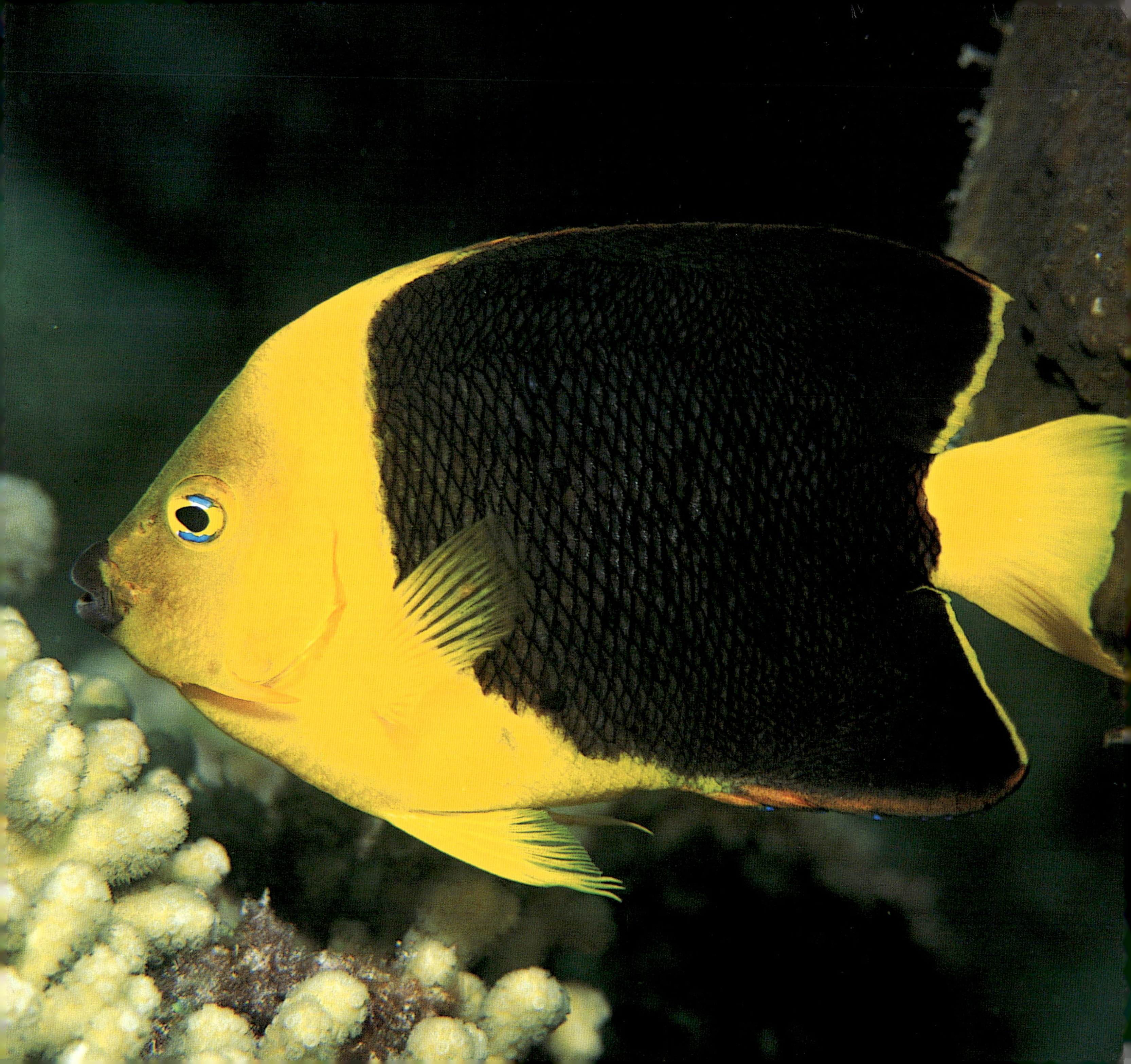

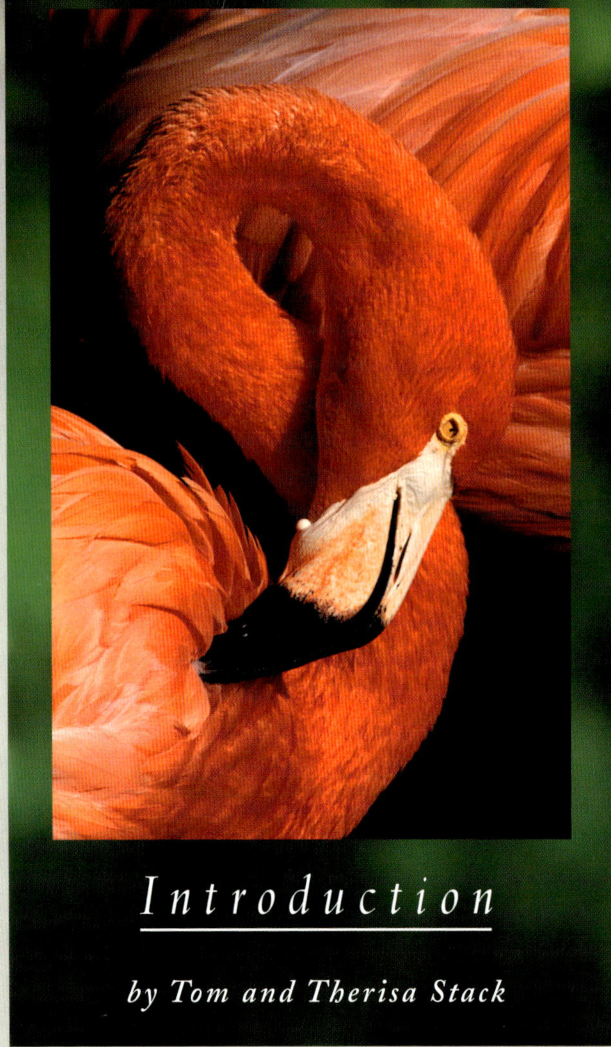

Introduction

by Tom and Therisa Stack

With the warm Gulf Stream waters to the east and the balmy Gulf of Mexico to the west, the Florida peninsula is a unique landscape that is the home of a multitude of wild creatures. Despite the state's relatively flat topography—most of the Florida's 65,758 square miles are at sea level, with the highest point only 345 feet—there are numerous ecosystems in which wildlife flourishes. Coral reefs, salt marshes, estuaries, mangroves, hardwood hammocks, pine forests, and freshwater springs are among the diverse habitats found in the Sunshine State. Few other states can claim to be home of not only birds and mammals, but also of whales, dolphins, manatees, alligators, crocodiles, coral polyps, and starfish. Simply put, wildlife abounds in Florida!

Often called a gateway to the tropics, the Florida peninsula serves as a migratory bird flyway. Bird lovers from around the world flock to the state during seasonal bird migration months, hoping to catch a glimpse of an elusive species.

Many of Florida's wildlife jewels are found beneath the surface of the ocean at Florida Keys National Marine Sanctuary on our continent's only living coral reef system. A vivid spectrum of living colors awaits those who snorkel or dive the crystalline waters off the Florida Keys. Even the less adventurous can experience the wonders of a coral reef from the safety of a glass-bottom boat at the John Pennekamp Coral Reef State Park in Key Largo. *But use caution: Our only living coral reefs are delicate and fragile, take only pictures and leave only bubbles.*

Environmental and ecological visionaries such as John James Audubon and Marjory Stoneman Douglas were instrumental in increasing public awareness of Florida's natural treasures. As a result, national parks, state parks, and wildlife refuges were established before commercial land development threatened many vital habitats. These preserves, often with boardwalks over wetland areas, provide unparalleled opportunities to view wild creatures in their natural environment.

Florida has three national parks: Everglades, Biscayne, and Dry Tortugas. Each plays a crucial role in protecting unique habitats critical for the survival of wildlife, including several endangered species.

Everglades National Park, on the southern tip of the Florida peninsula between Miami and Naples, is the largest remaining subtropical wilderness area in the continental United States. Here fresh water flows in a broad, shallow band from Lake Okeechobee some 120 miles south to Florida Bay. This "river of grass" and its tributaries provide a haven for a multitude of wildlife, including the endangered Florida panther, American crocodile, and West Indian manatee. So important is Everglades habitat that it was designated an International Biosphere Reserve and a World Heritage Site.

Biscayne National Park, located in the shadows of Miami, protects the northernmost section of the only coral reef in the continental United States. While bird watching is very popular, some of the most unique creatures of Biscayne National Park can be observed while snorkeling or diving its dazzling underwater reefs offshore.

Some 65 miles southwest of Key West, Dry Tortugas National Park is remote and difficult to reach, but well worth the trip. Terns and frigate birds nest here on small, sandy island sanctuaries nestled in turquoise waters.

Florida state parks and national wildlife refuges are real gems for wildlife viewing. Many of the images in this book came from these unique preserves.

Homosassa Springs Wildlife State Park, north of Tampa, is the best place to view manatees up close and personal. The park's floating observatory offers visitors an underwater view of these gentle giants surrounded by immense schools of freshwater fish.

Myakka River State Park, with extensive boardwalks over pristine wetlands and prairies, is an excellent place to observe birds and alligators on misty mornings. Be sure to traverse the unique canopy walkway through the hammock treetops.

The serene Loxahatchee River, a federally designated Wild and Scenic River, flows through Jonathan Dickinson State Park just south of Stuart, Florida. Wildlife here can best be observed by drifting quietly downstream in a kayak or canoe.

The Merritt Island National Wildlife refuge, adjacent to the Kennedy Space Center, provides sanctuary for more than 300 species of birds. The Black Point Wildlife Drive is a prime location for viewing crimson roseate spoonbills, soaring bald eagles, and countless egrets and herons. Vast flocks of migratory waterfowl descend on the wetlands here during the winter months.

On Sanibel Island off Florida's west coast, the J. N. "Ding" Darling National Wildlife Refuge boasts a five-mile wildlife drive through an estuarine habitat. Visitors—from the safety of their cars—can view lurking alligators and numerous species of birds wading at the base of mangrove roots.

Fort DeSoto County Park on Mullet Key, at the entrance to Tampa Bay, is a superior location to view returning migratory birds from March through May.

Shore birds and wading birds are common along the pristine sandy beaches there year round.

Florida is an outstanding location to visit and view wildlife. Shrug off the workaday world and take time to explore the state's diverse habitats and experience the fascinating creatures that reside there. Remember that wildlife is wild, and we are merely privileged visitors to their home.

If you've picked up this book, you share our love for wildlife and nature. Together we hold the key to safeguarding the future of Florida's wildlife.

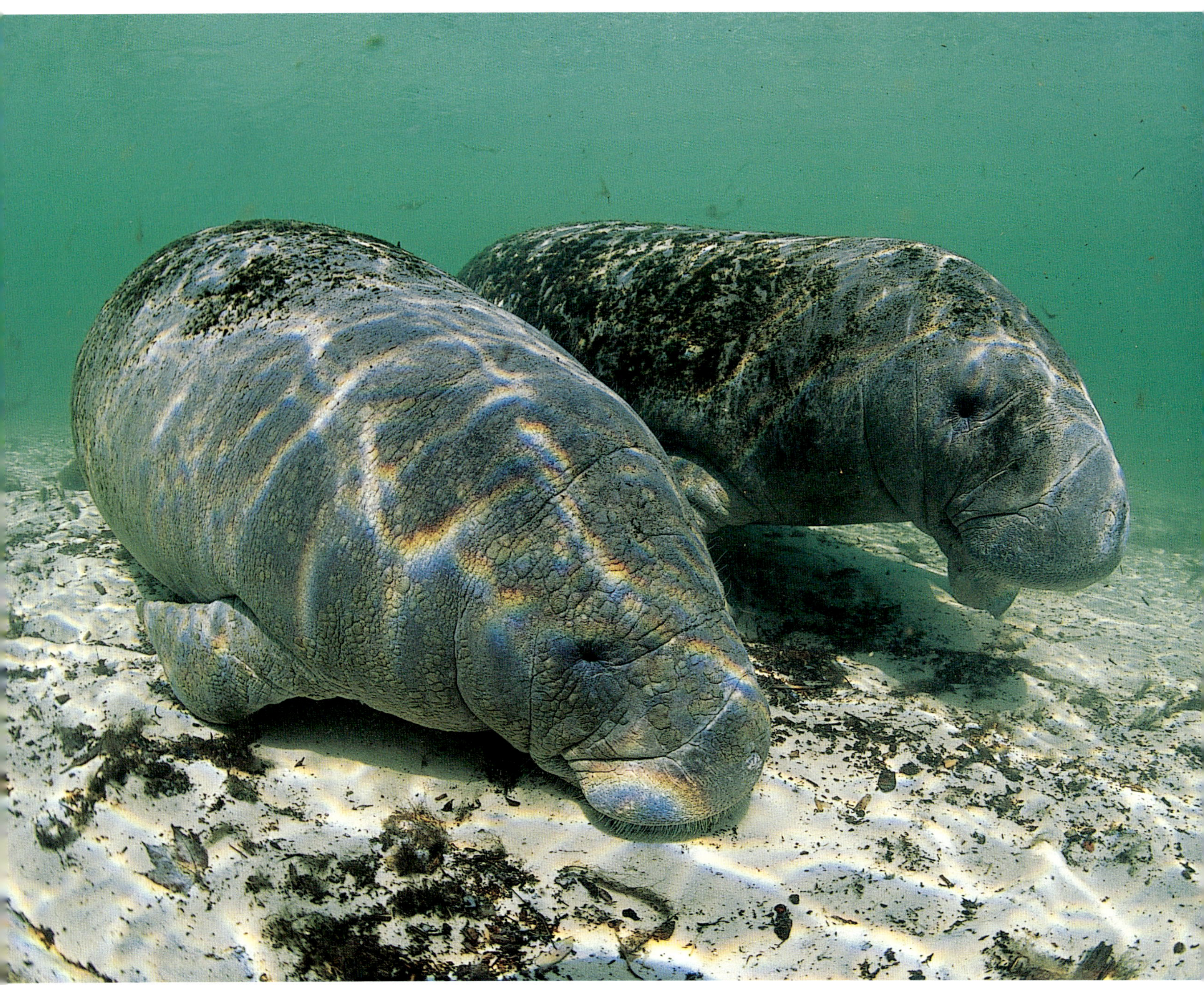

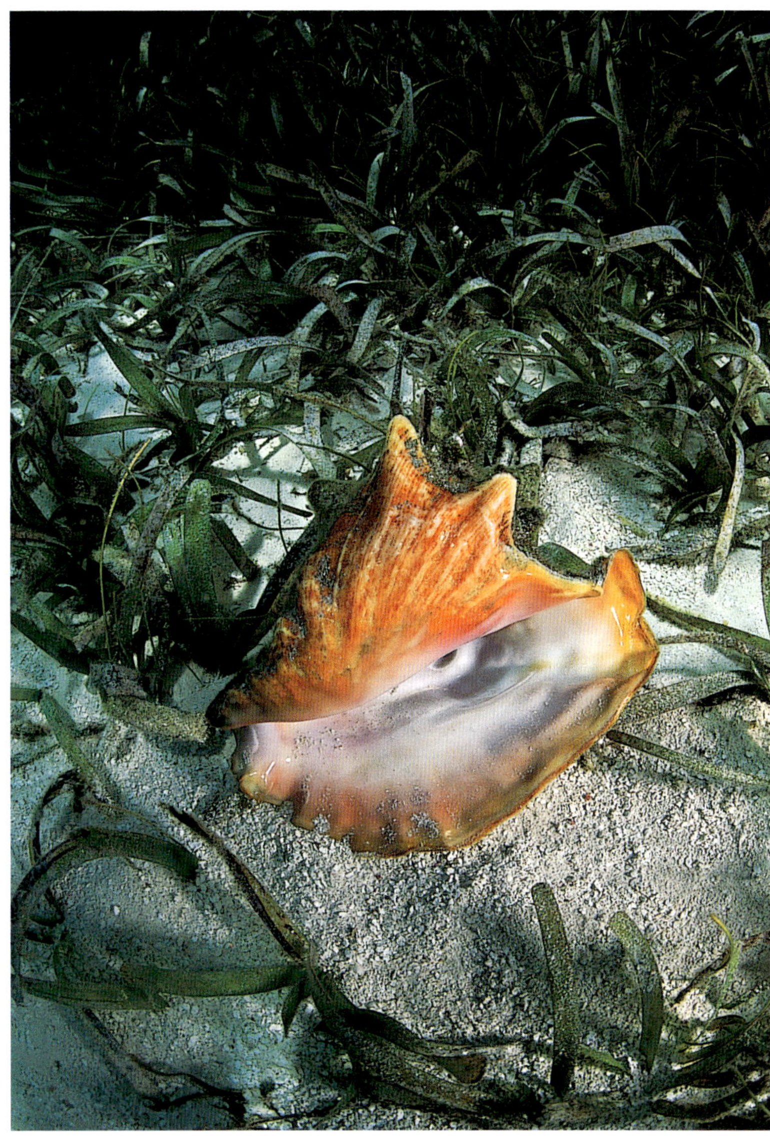

LEFT: After years of protection, the numbers of queen conches are increasing throughout the Florida Keys.

FAR LEFT: A pair of manatees basks in the warm, shallow waters of the Homosassa River.

RIGHT: An egret warily eyes a white-tailed deer wading through wetlands at Shark Valley in Everglades National Park.

BELOW: A red-shouldered hawk surveys its surroundings at Myakka River State Park.

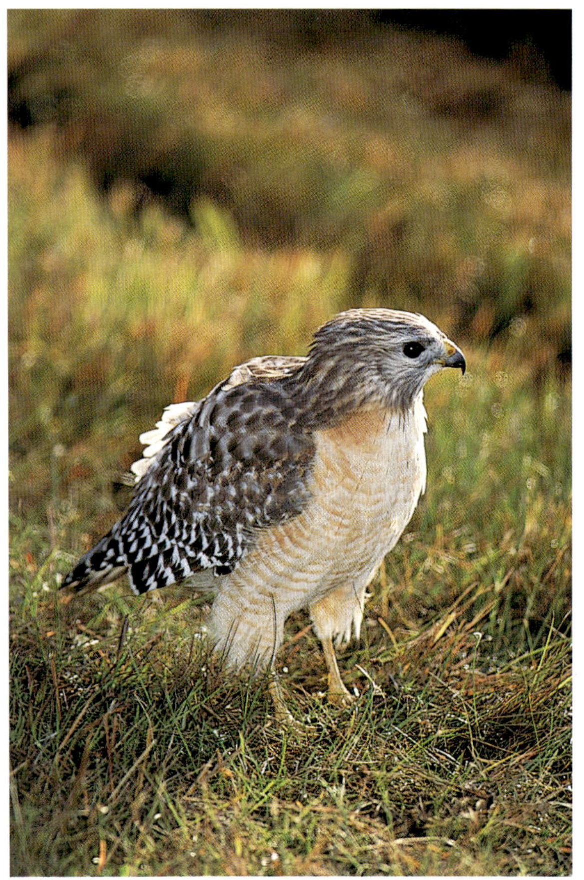

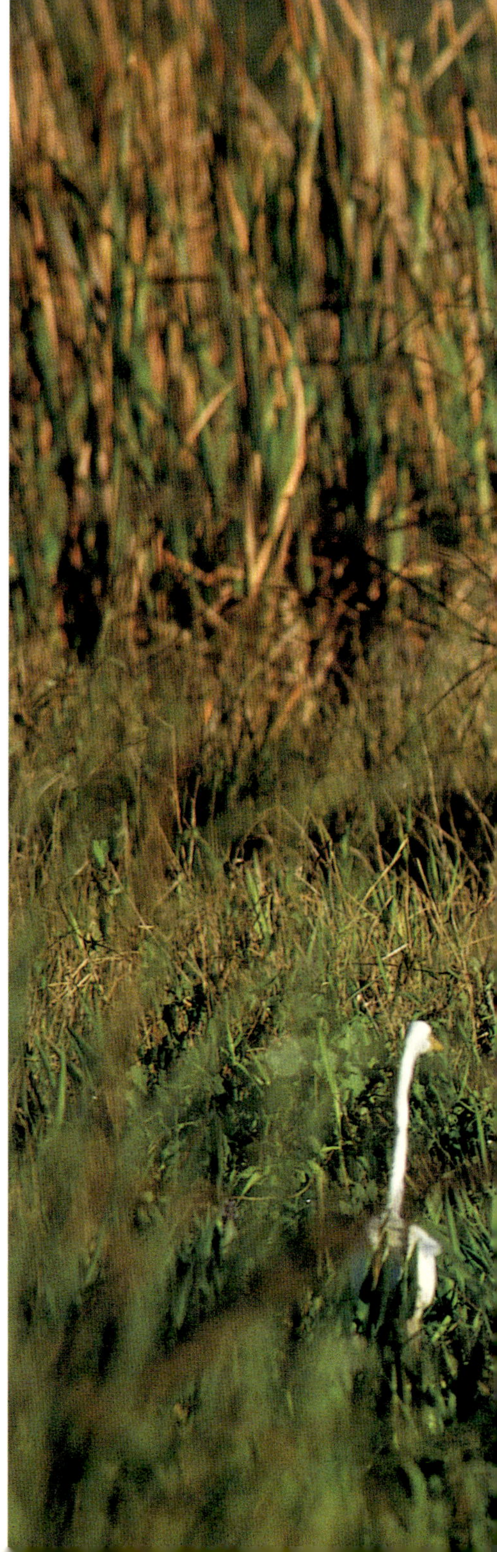

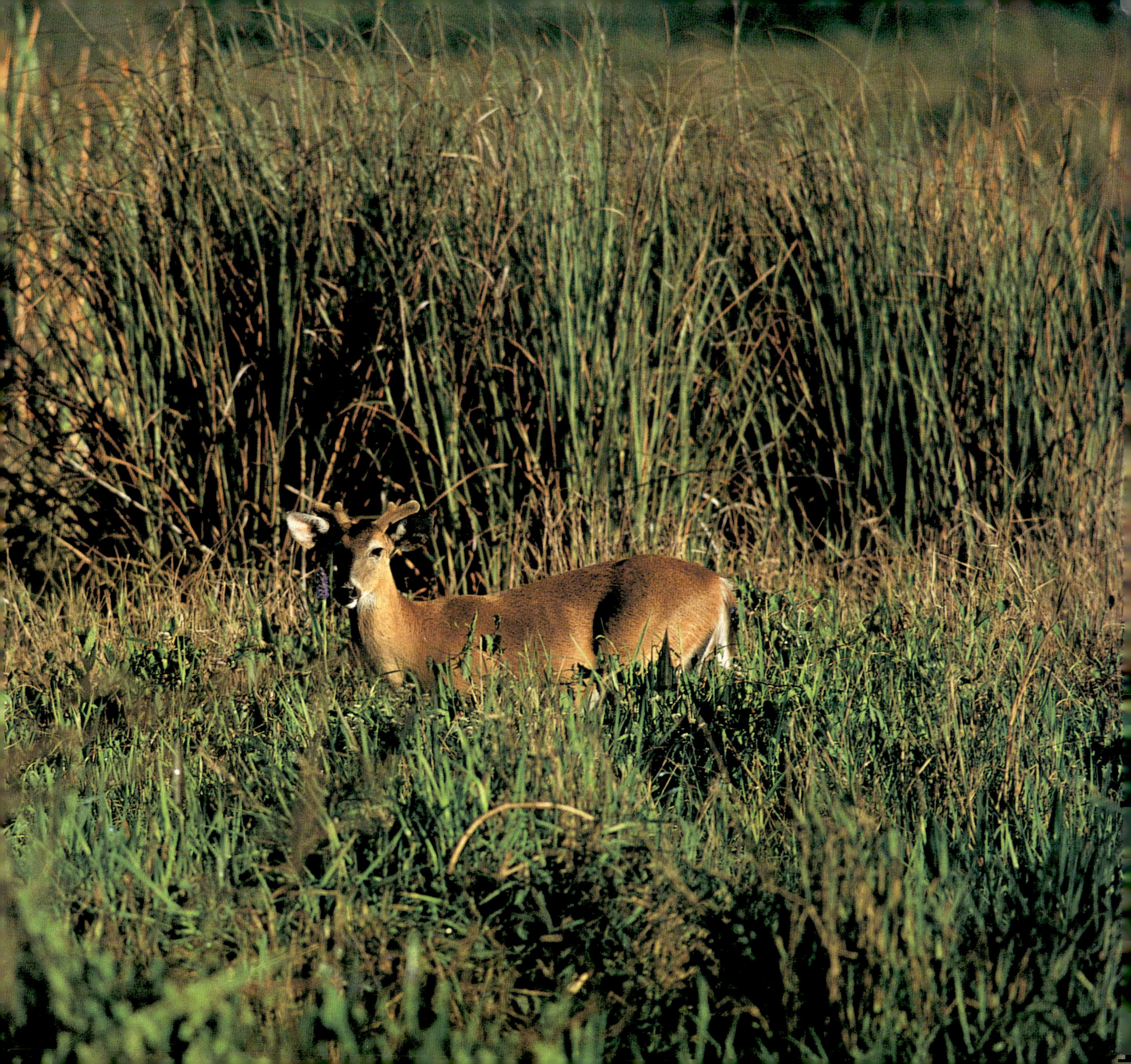

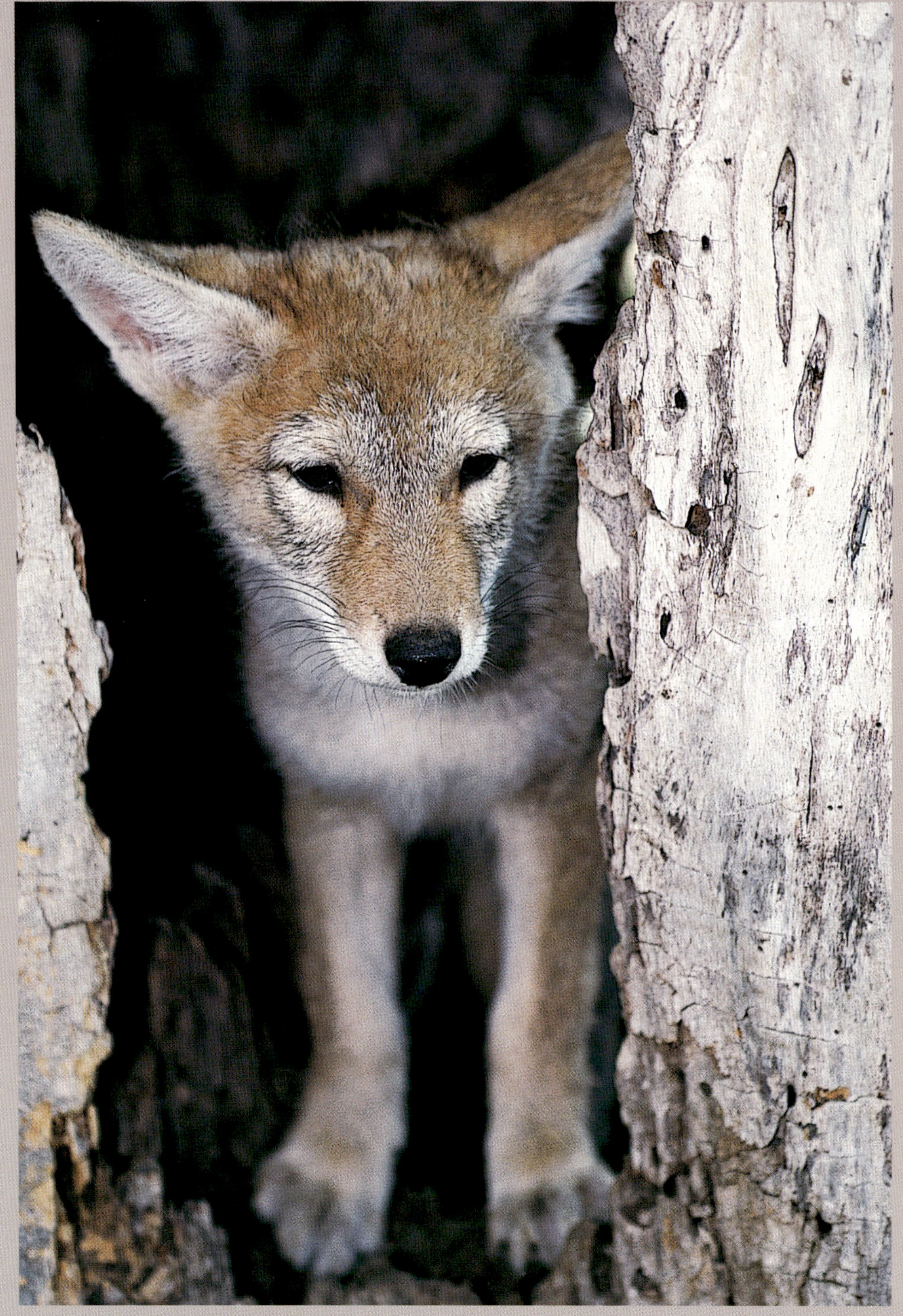

FACING PAGE: A coyote pup peeks out from its den in a dead tree.

BELOW: Opossums are nocturnal marsupials common throughout Florida.

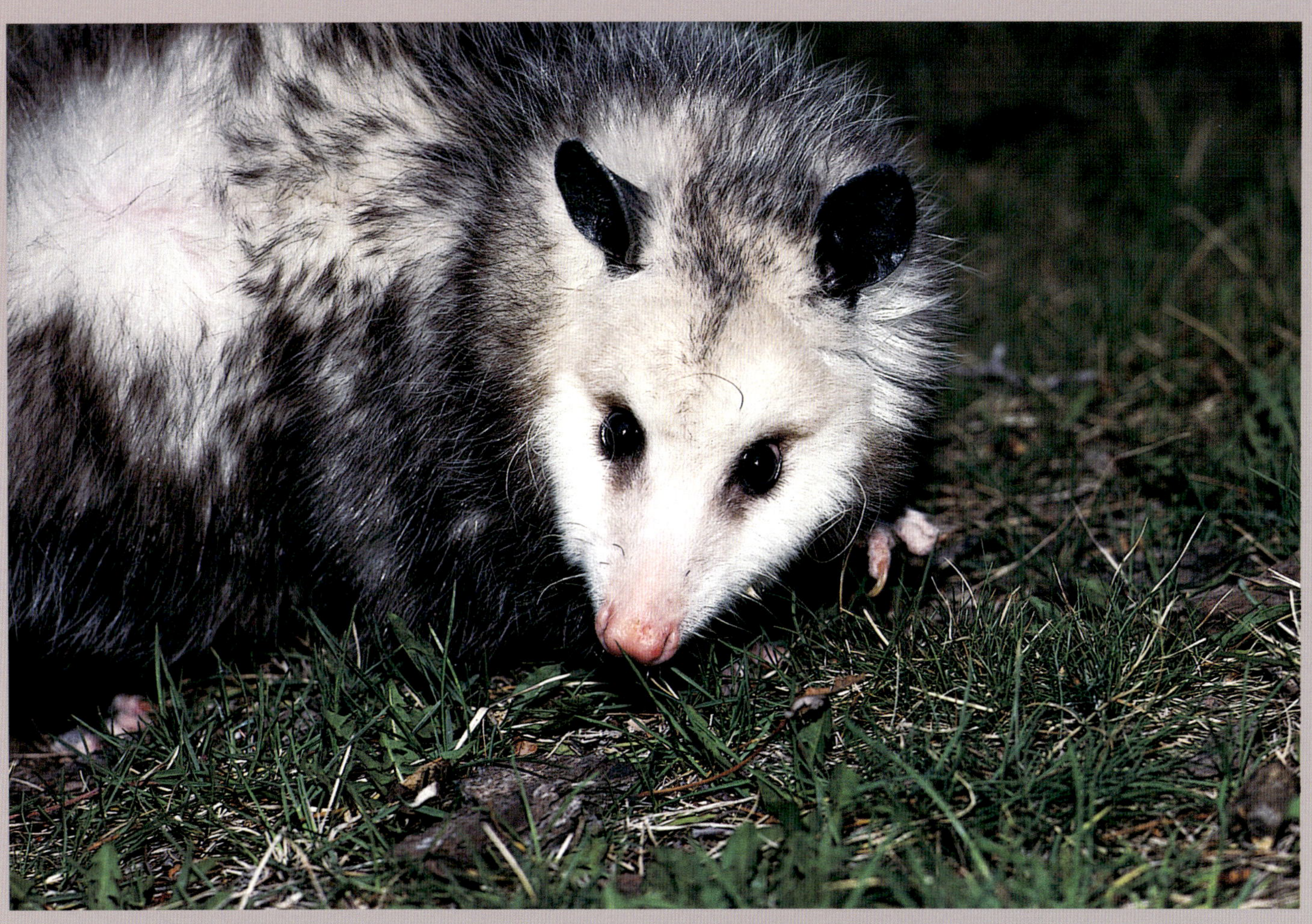

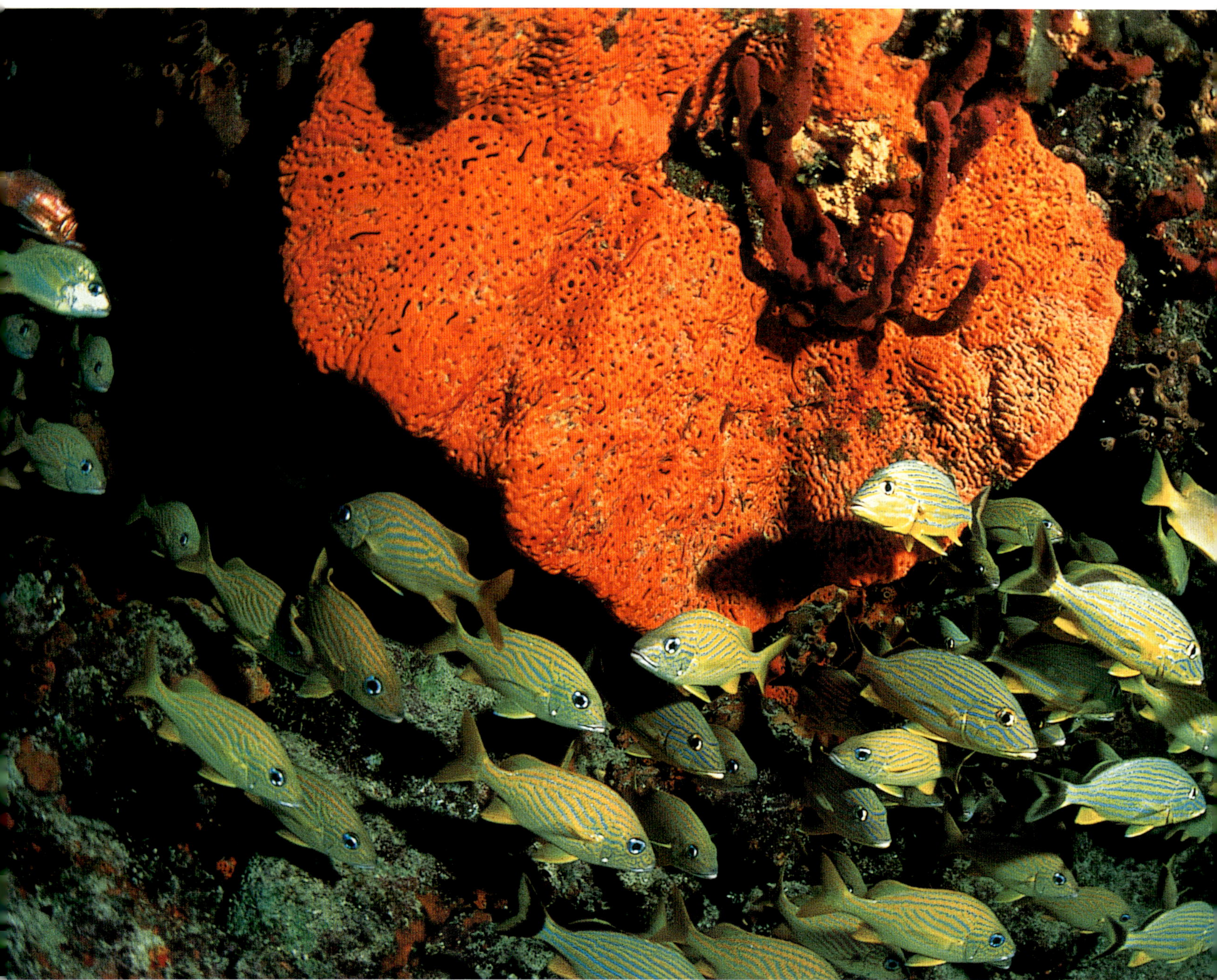

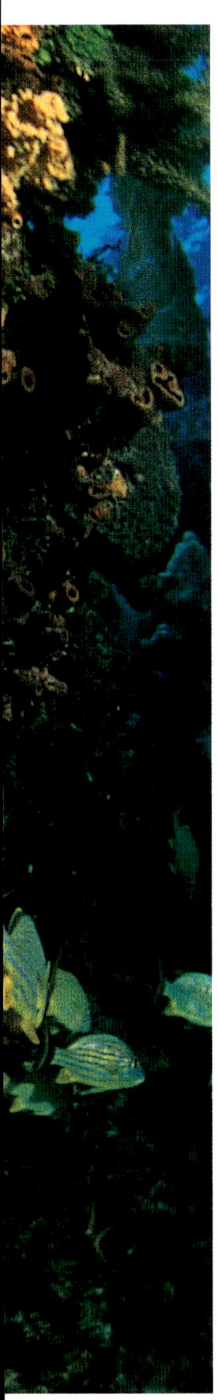

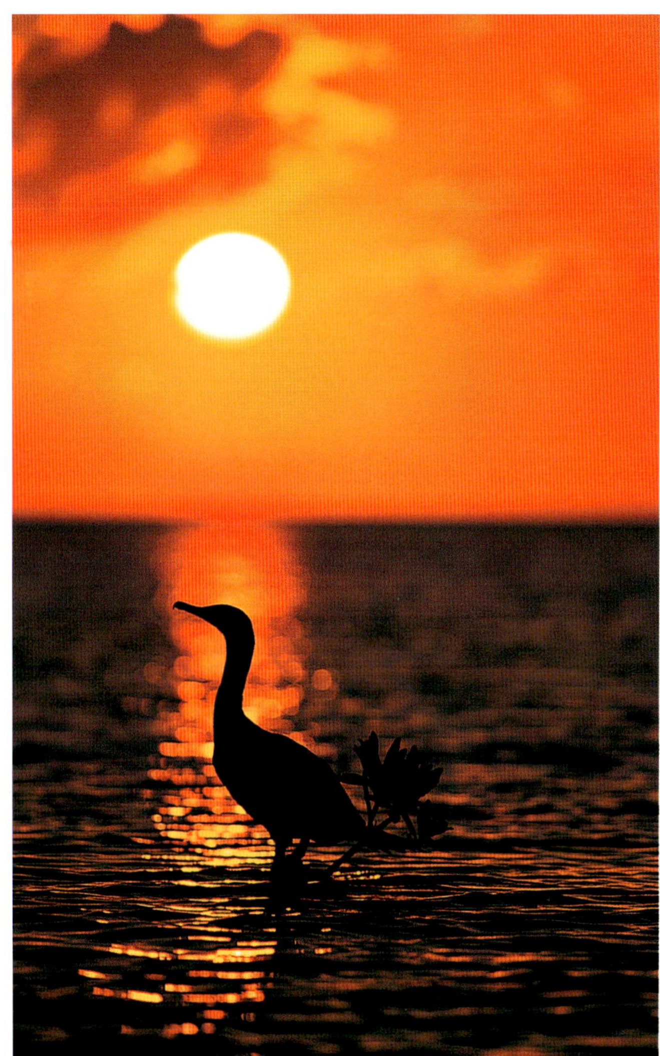

LEFT: A double-crested cormorant basks in the waning warmth of the setting sun in Everglades National Park.

FAR LEFT: Blue striped grunts swim beneath brightly colored sponges at Molasses Reef off Key Largo.

RIGHT: Increasingly rare, black bears still inhabit various parts of Florida, particularly the Ocala National Forest.

BELOW: The indigo snake is classified as a threatened species. Non-poisonous and gentle, indigo snakes can sometimes be observed foraging during the daytime. JOE MCDONALD/TOM STACK & ASSOCIATES

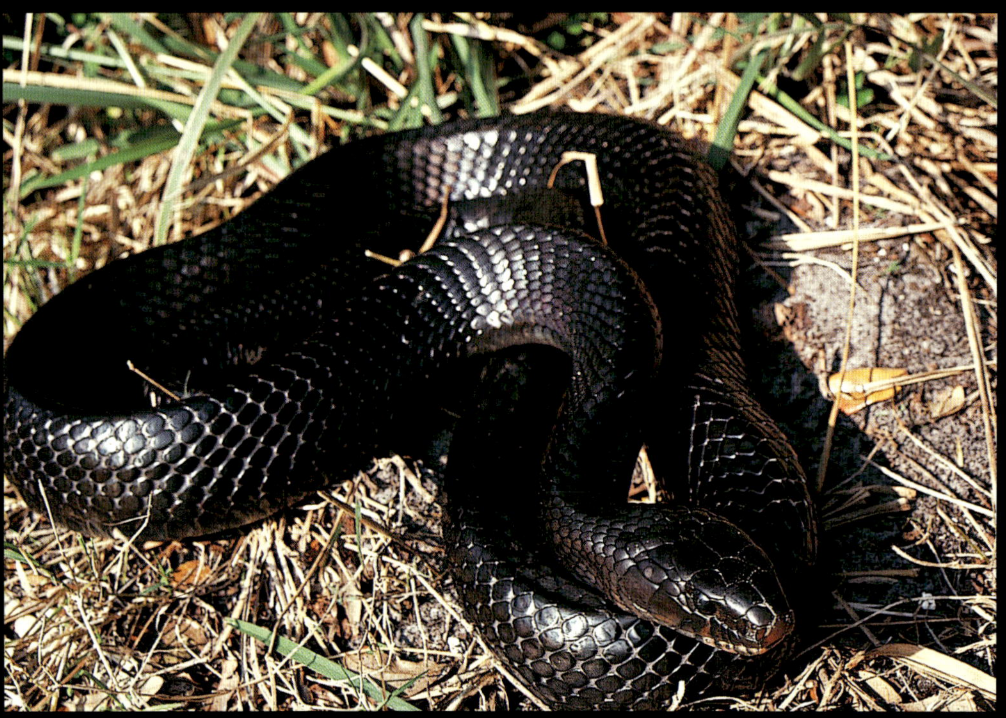

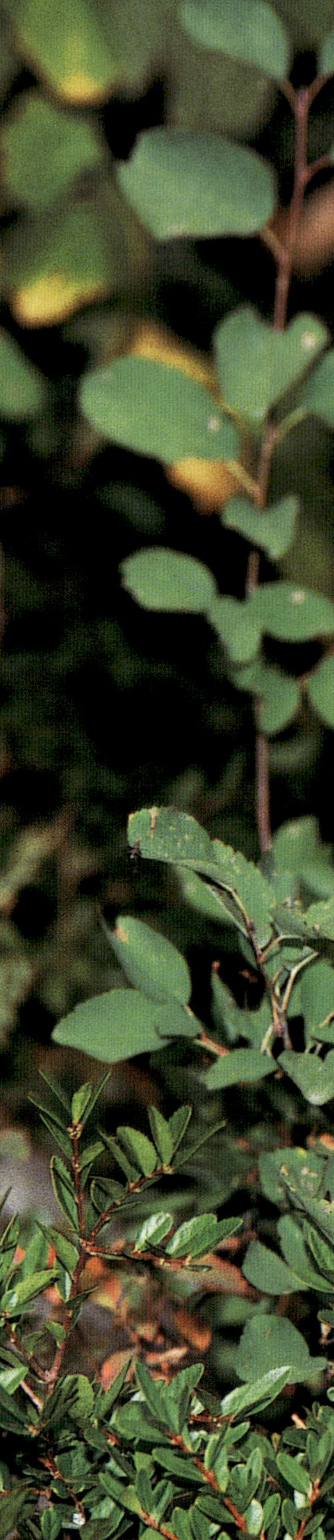

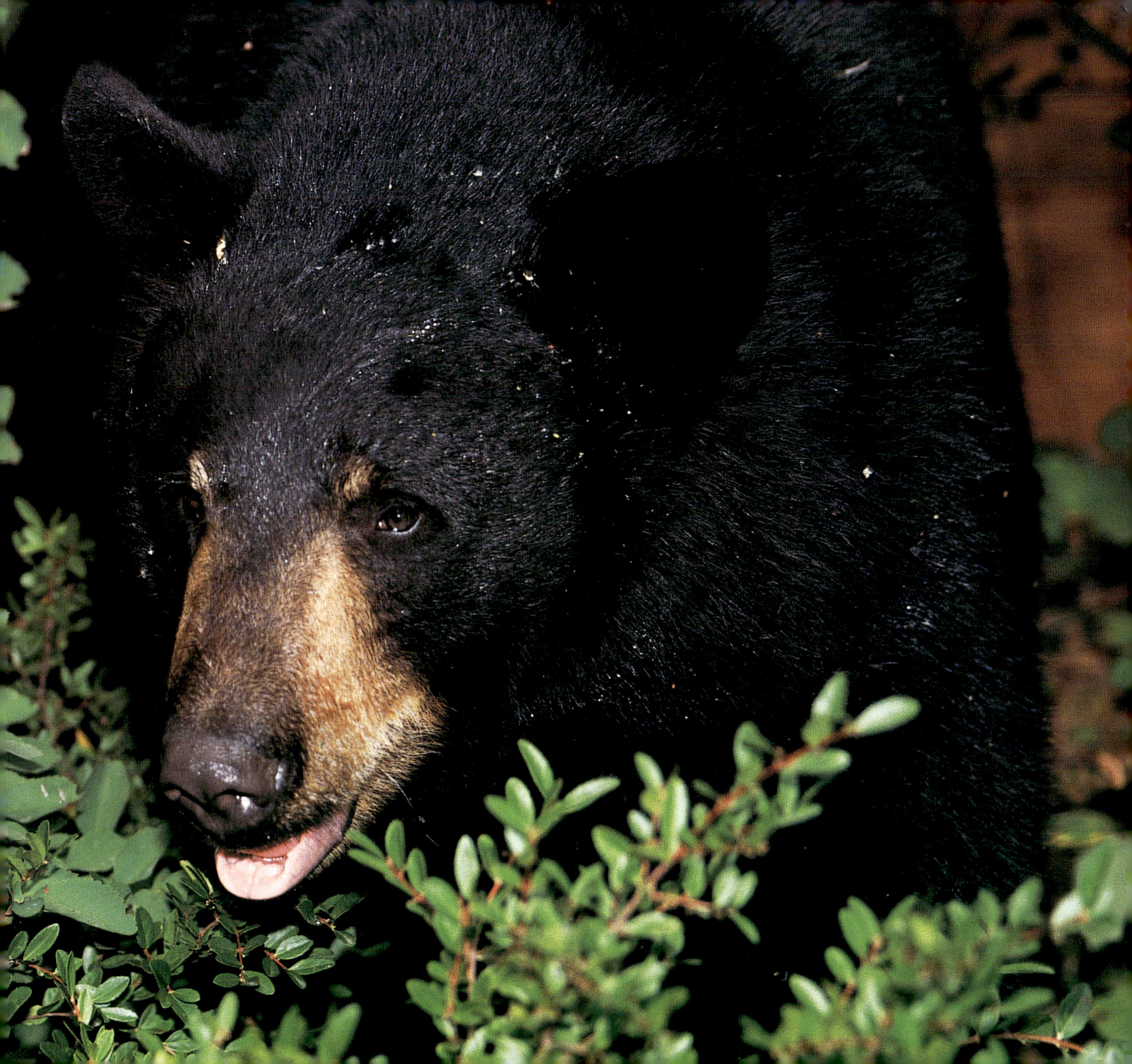

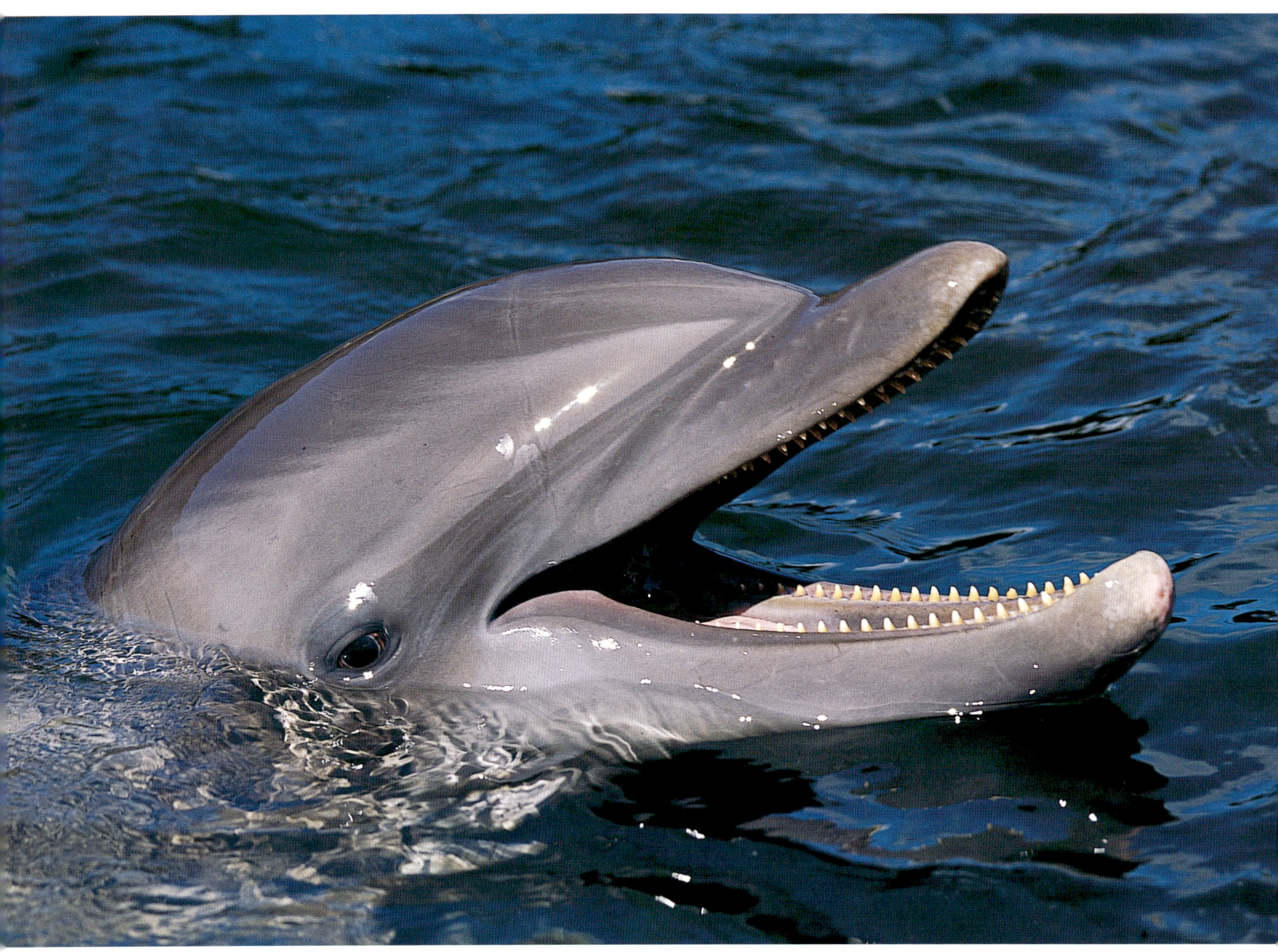

Highly intelligent and curious, Atlantic bottlenose dolphins frequent Florida waters.

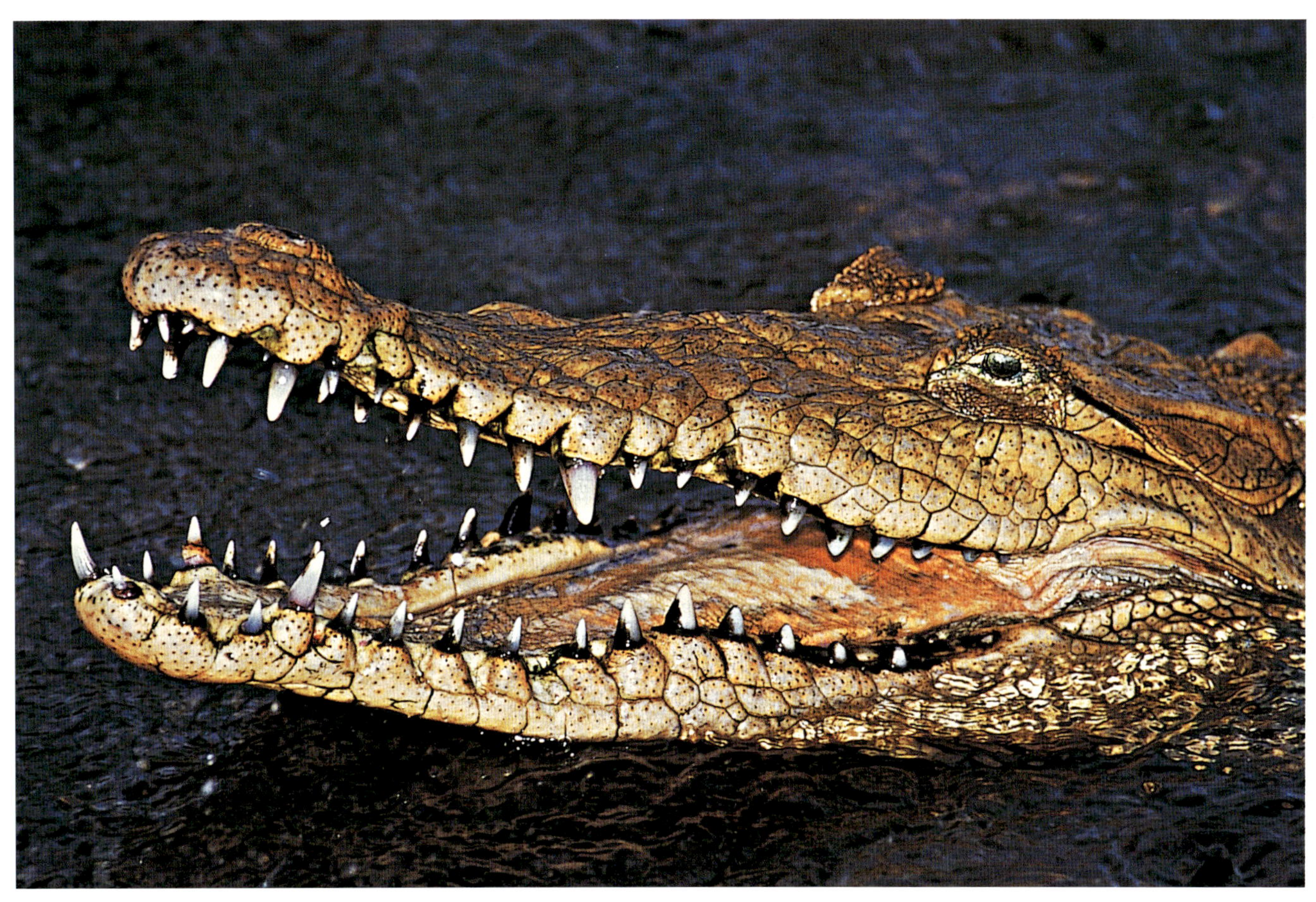

American crocodiles are an endangered species best viewed in the wild near the Flamingo Visitor Center in Everglades National Park.

RIGHT: A tricolored heron perches at J. N. "Ding" Darling National Wildlife Refuge on Sanibel Island.

FAR RIGHT: An introduced species, Cuban tree frogs are now fairly common throughout Florida. This one is using its toe pads to grip the branch of a sea grape tree.

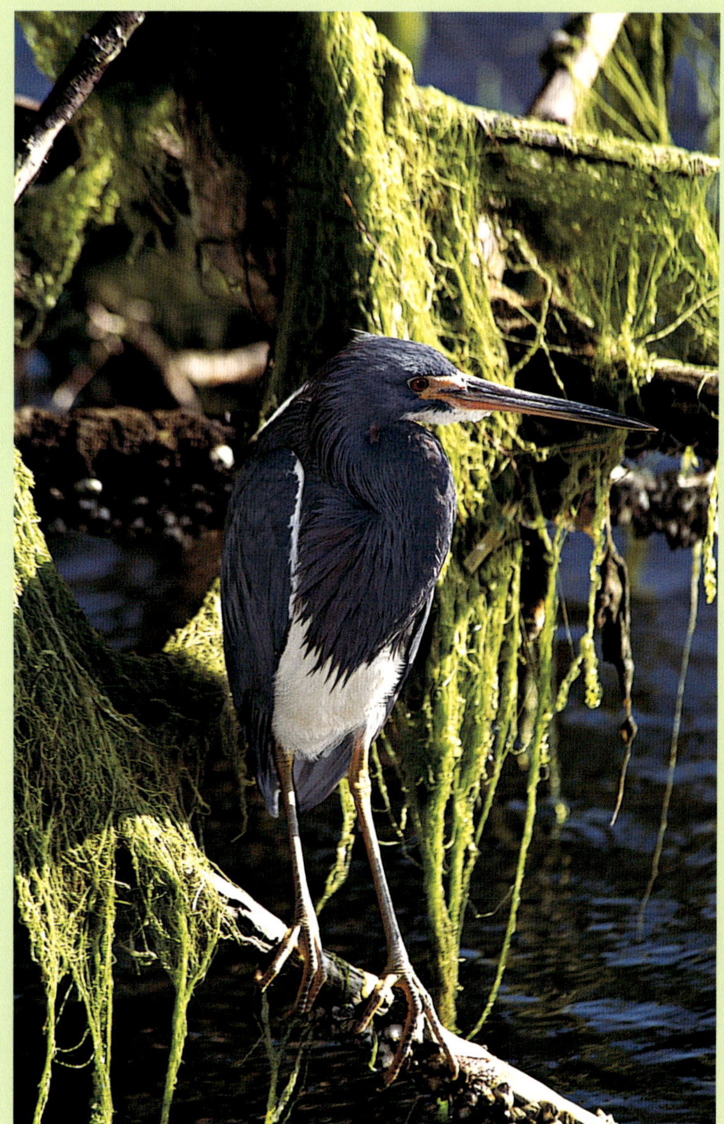

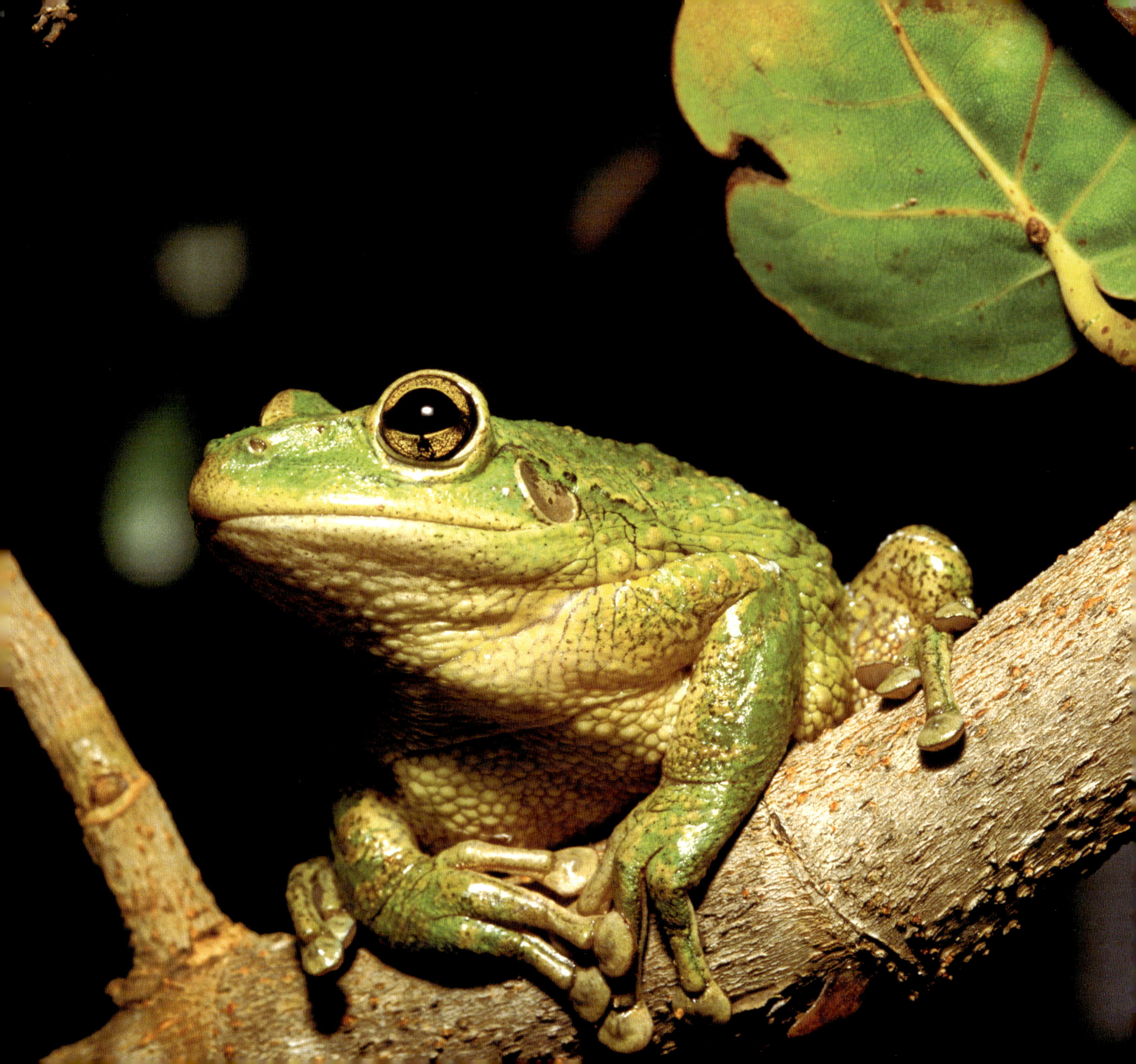

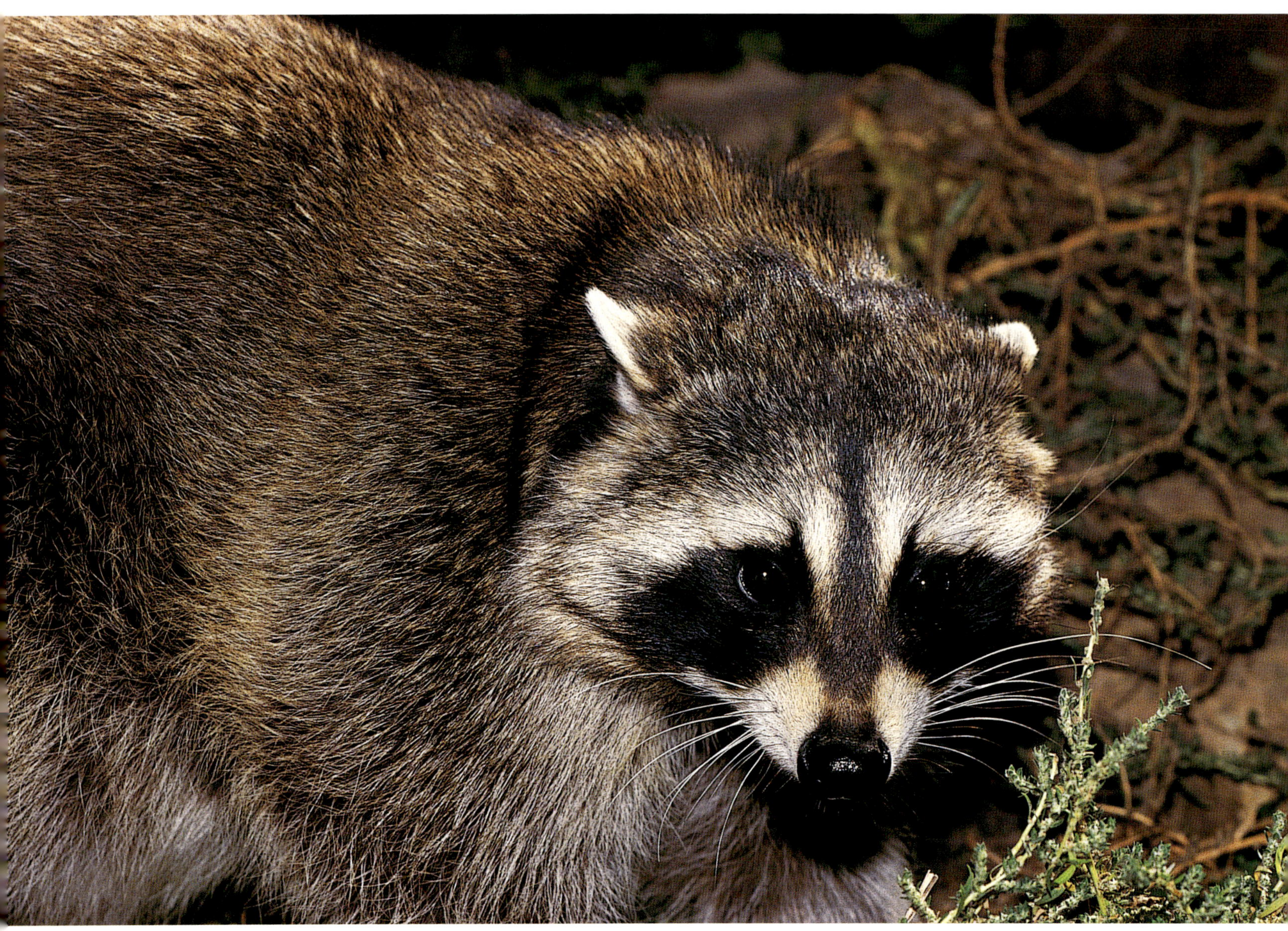

Like a masked bandit, a raccoon forages during the night.

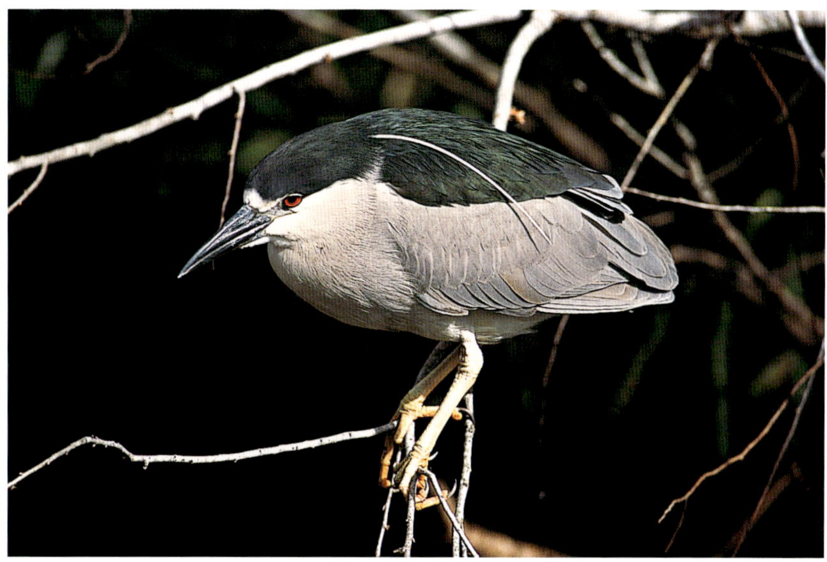

ABOVE: A black-crowned night heron patiently waits for its next meal to swim by.

RIGHT: A gray fox kit. The gray fox is common throughout mainland Florida but is seldom seen due to its secretive behavior.

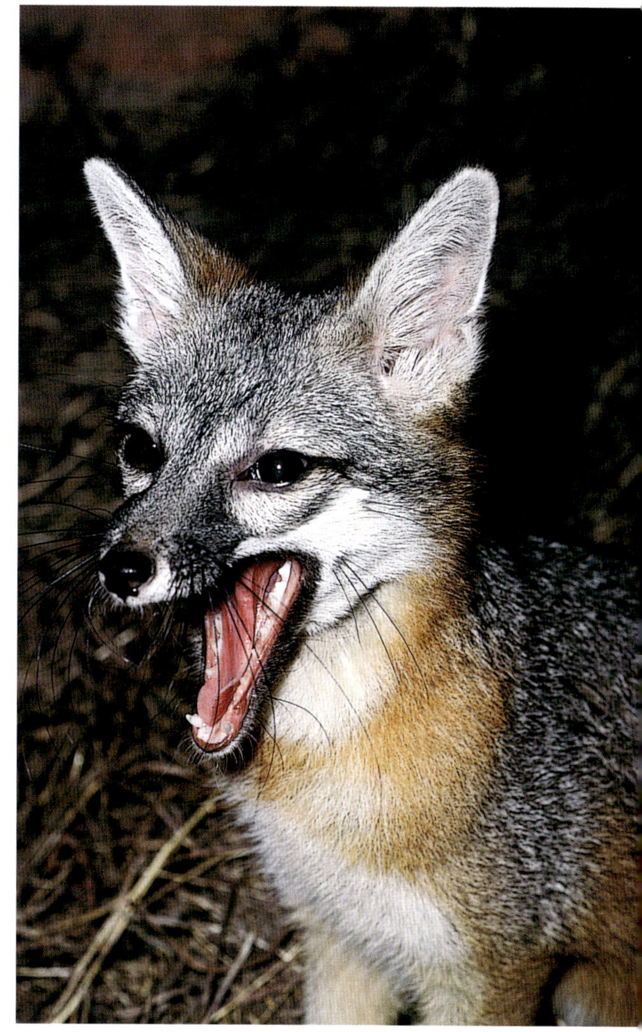

RIGHT: At the Merritt Island National Wildlife Refuge near Titusville, a roseate spoonbill and white ibis feed in the shallows together.

BELOW: A wading greater flamingo feeds by sweeping its head back and forth and filtering water through its beak.

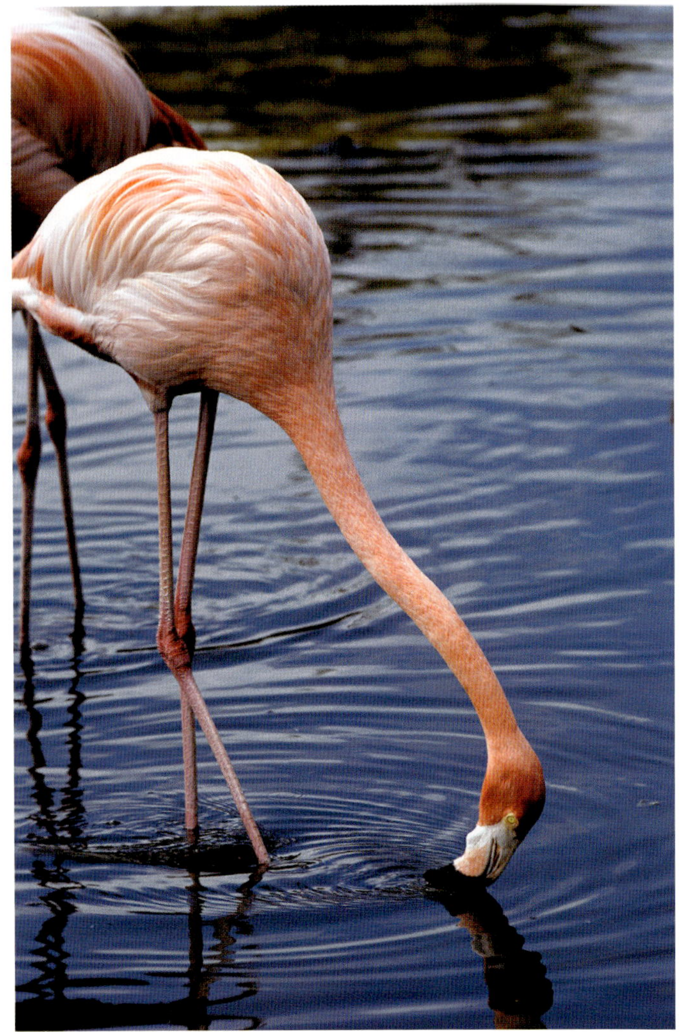

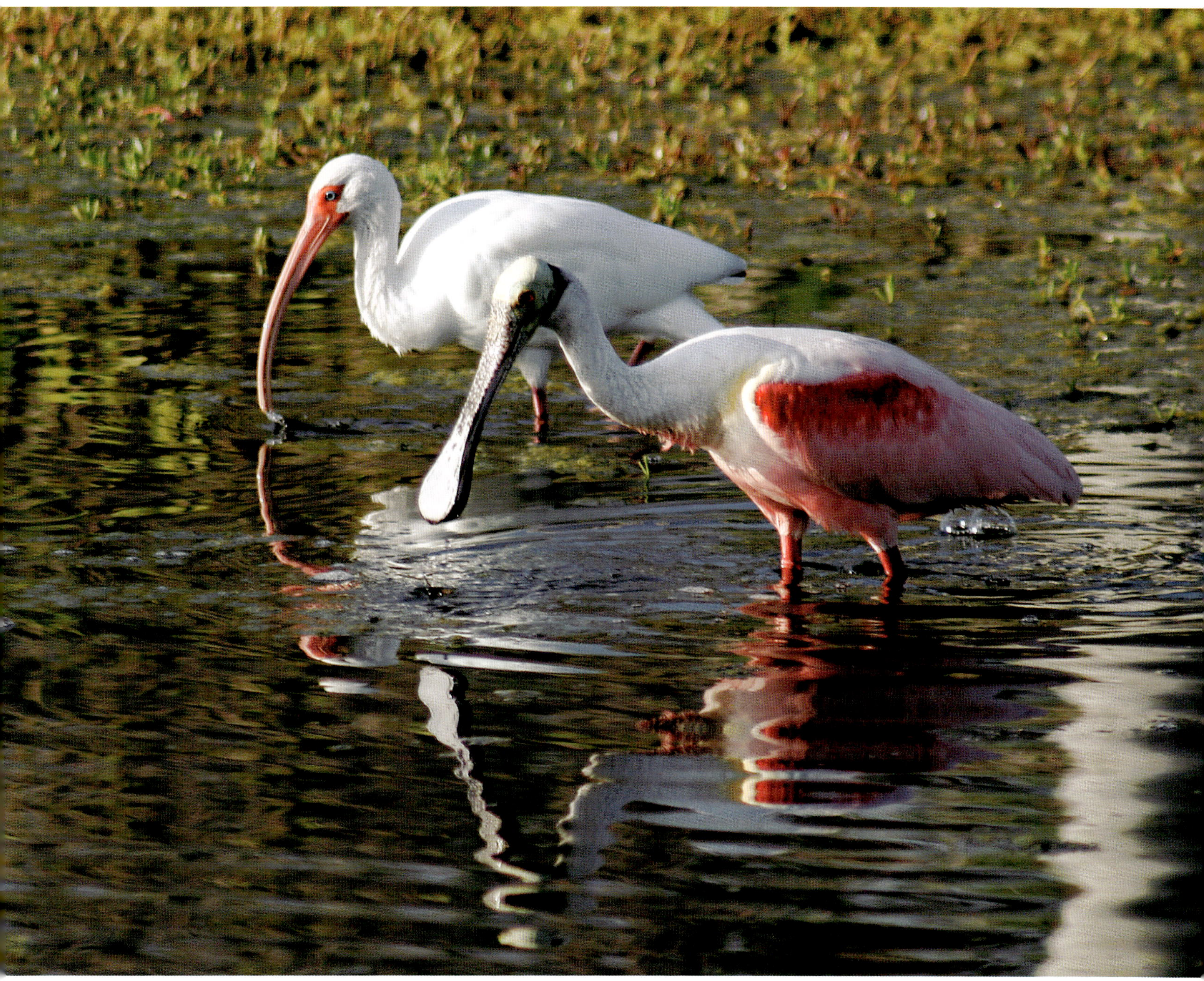

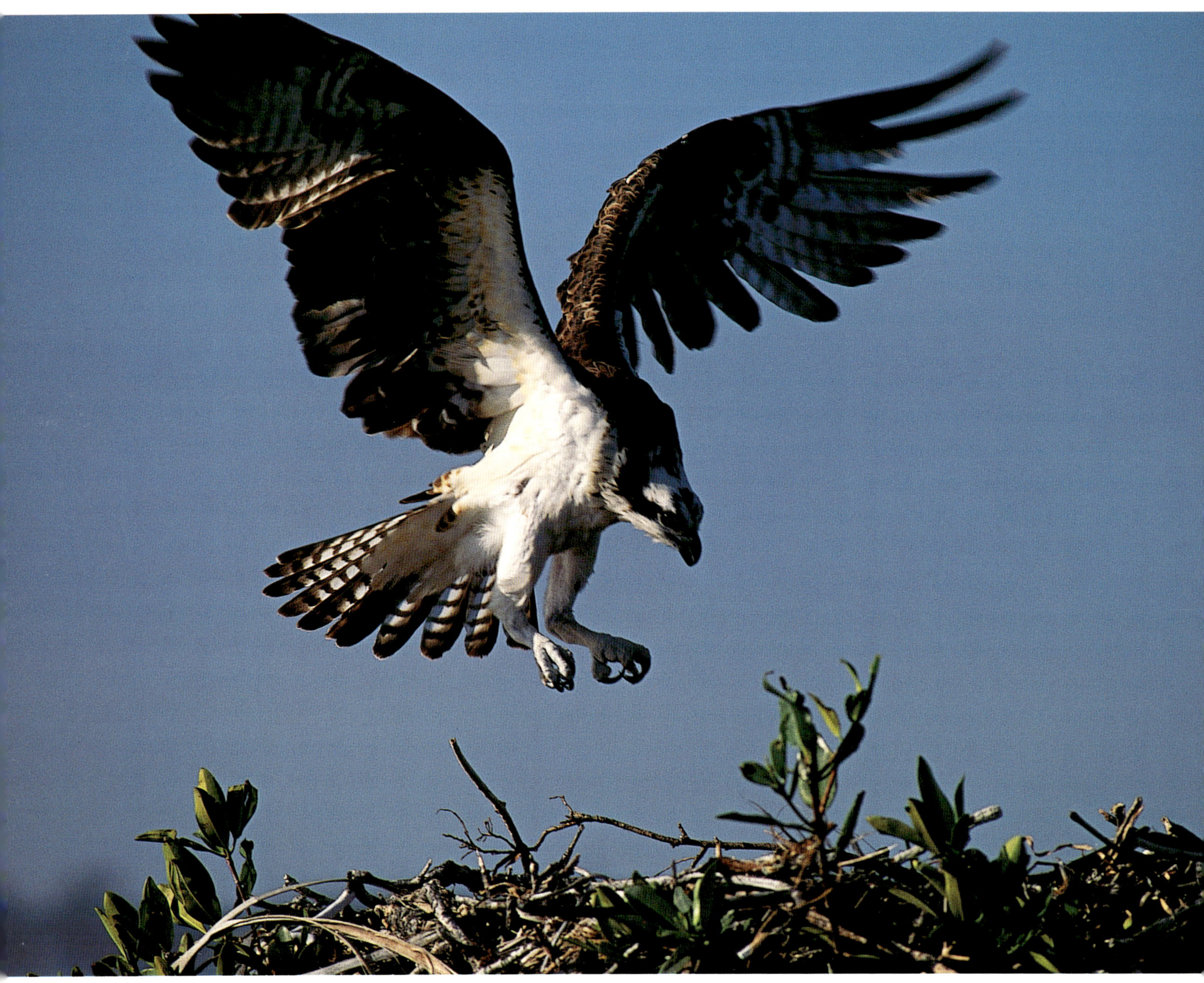

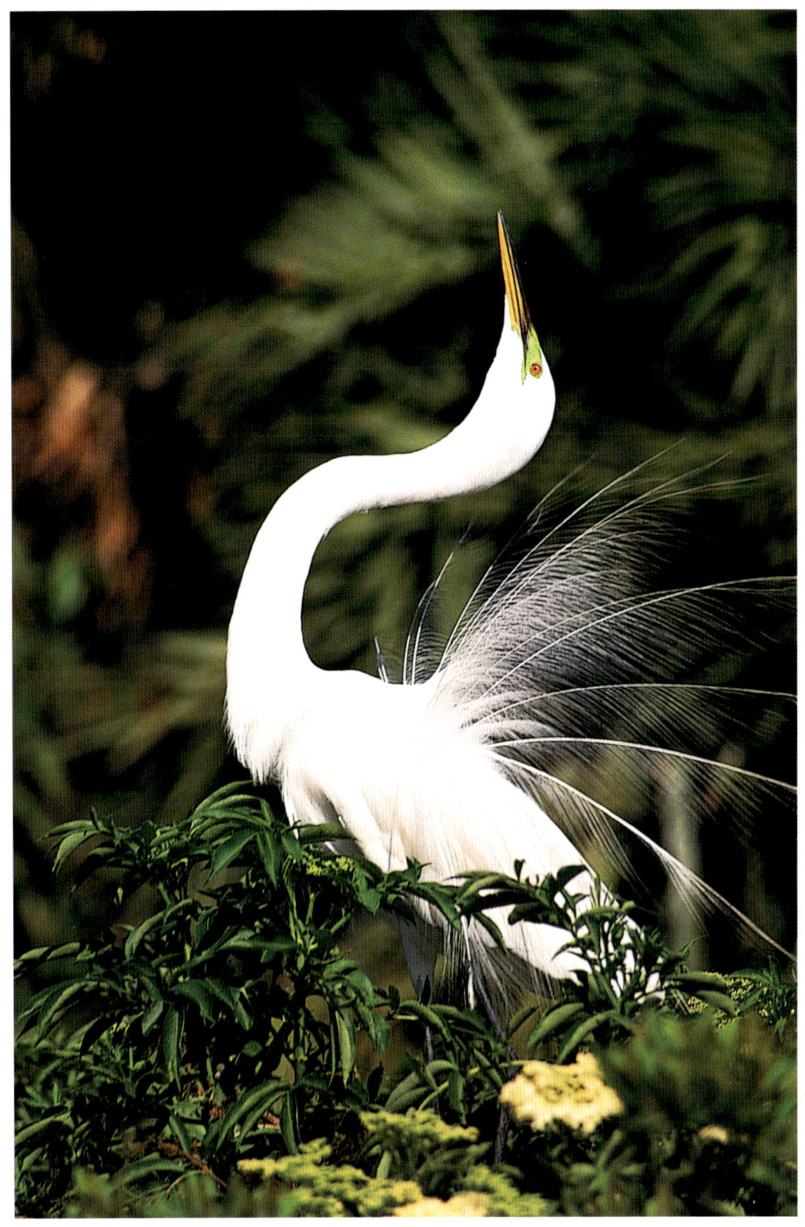

LEFT: This male great egret proudly displays his breeding plumage at a rookery.

FACING PAGE: An osprey prepares to land in its nest in Everglades National Park.

RIGHT: Duckweed provides camouflage for a stealthy American alligator in Corkscrew Swamp Sanctuary outside Naples.

BELOW: Green iguanas, introduced into South Florida as escaped or released pets, are now very common. Many Florida homeowners occasionally lose fruit and flowers to iguanas.

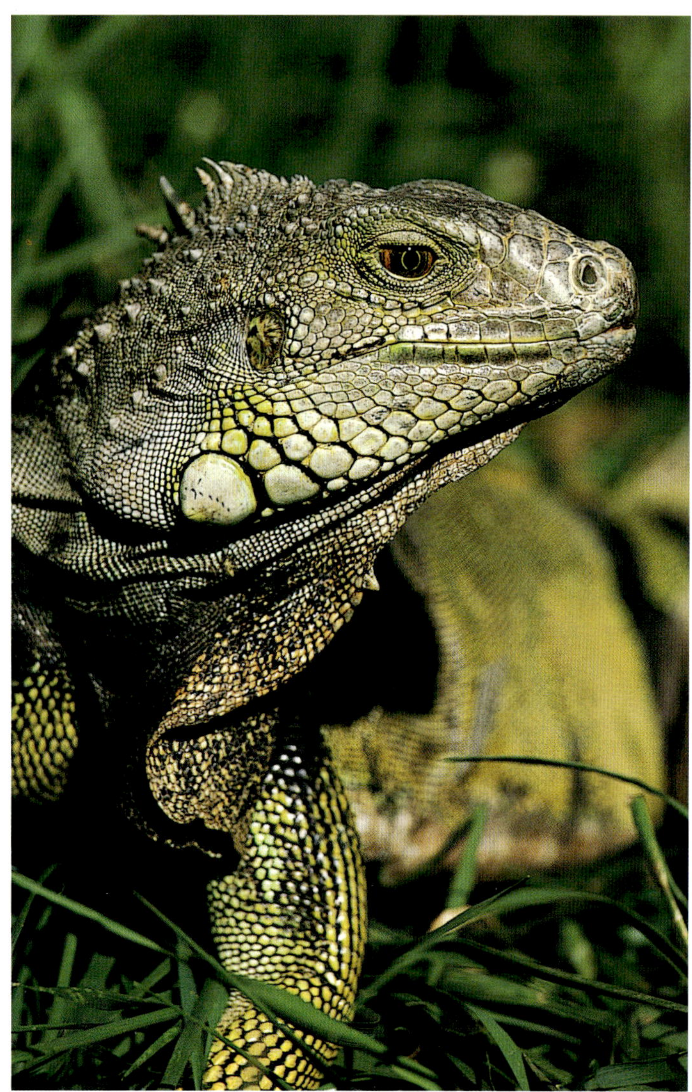

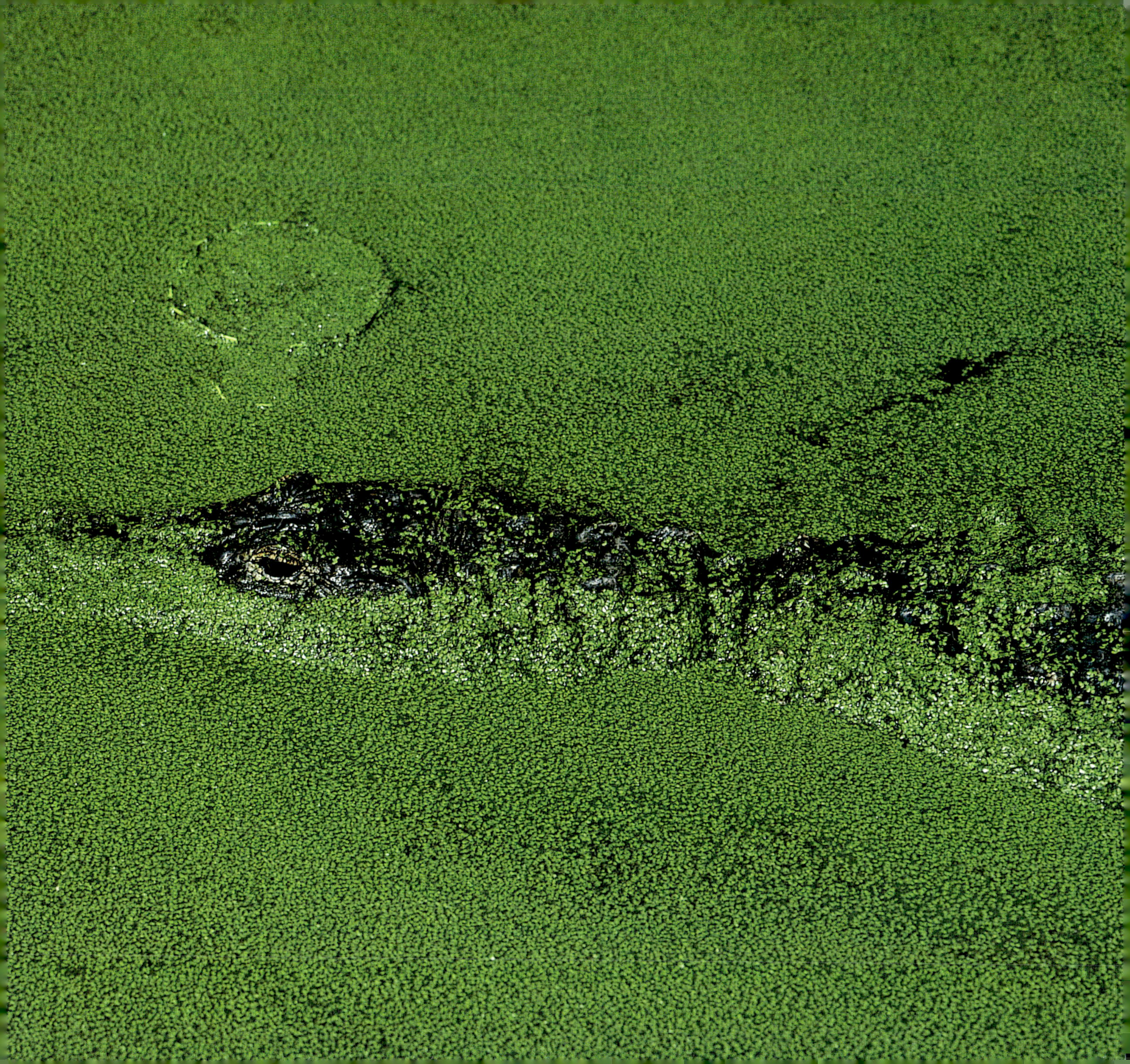

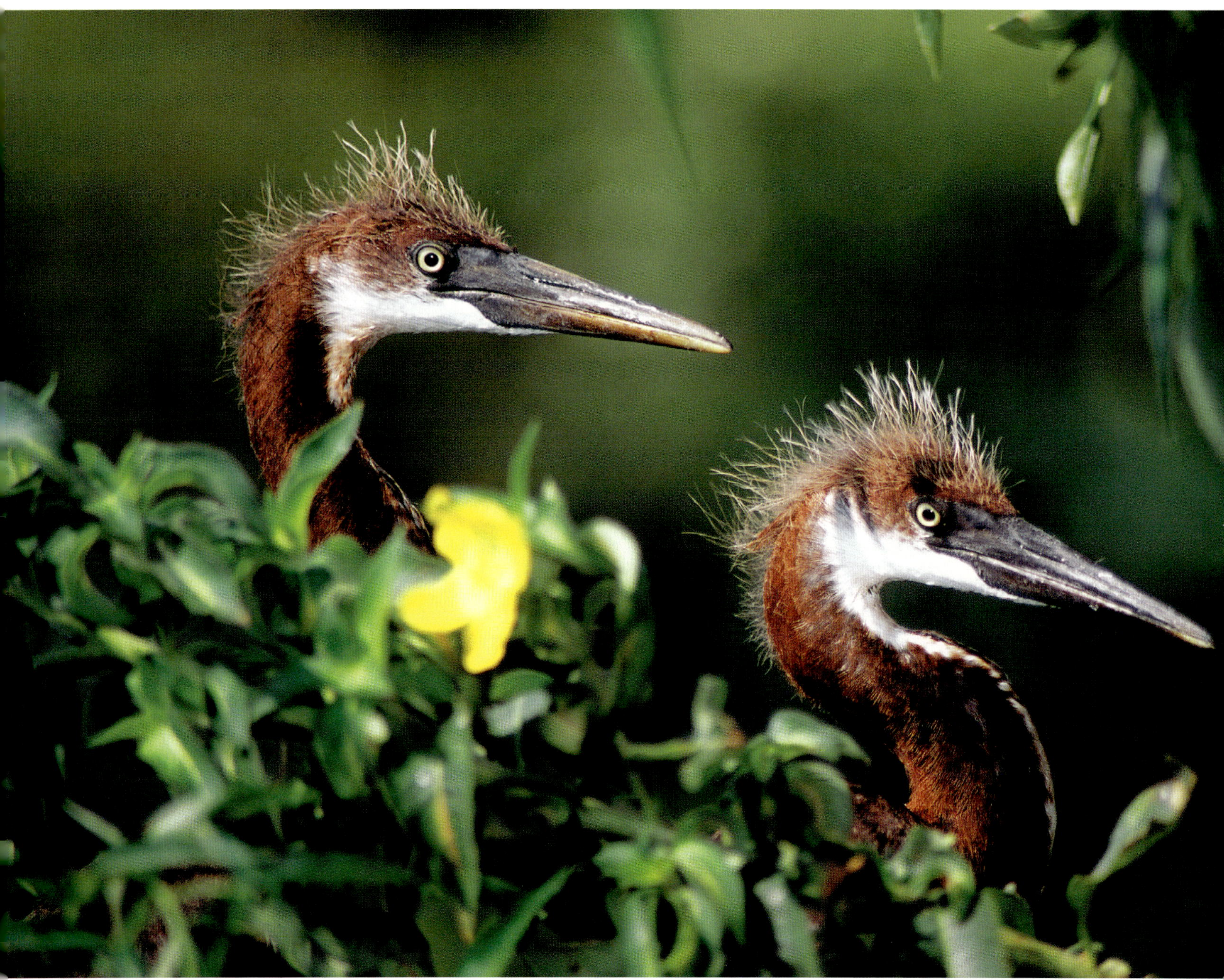

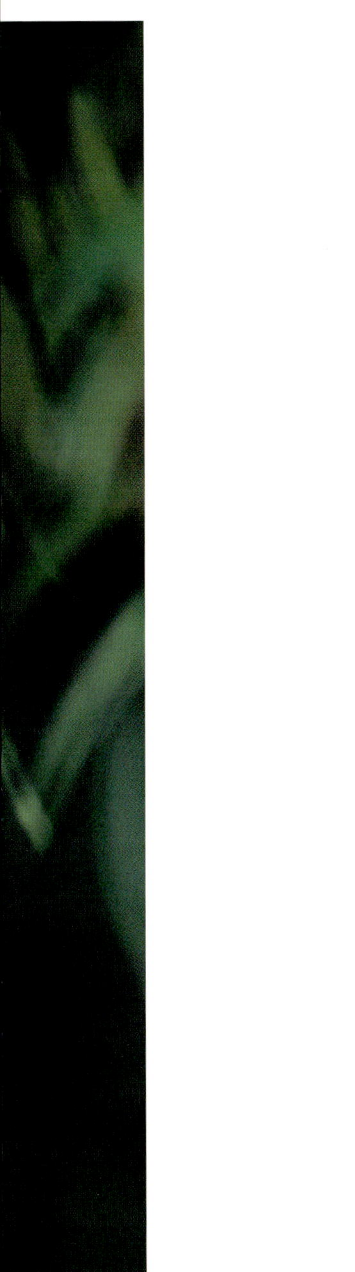

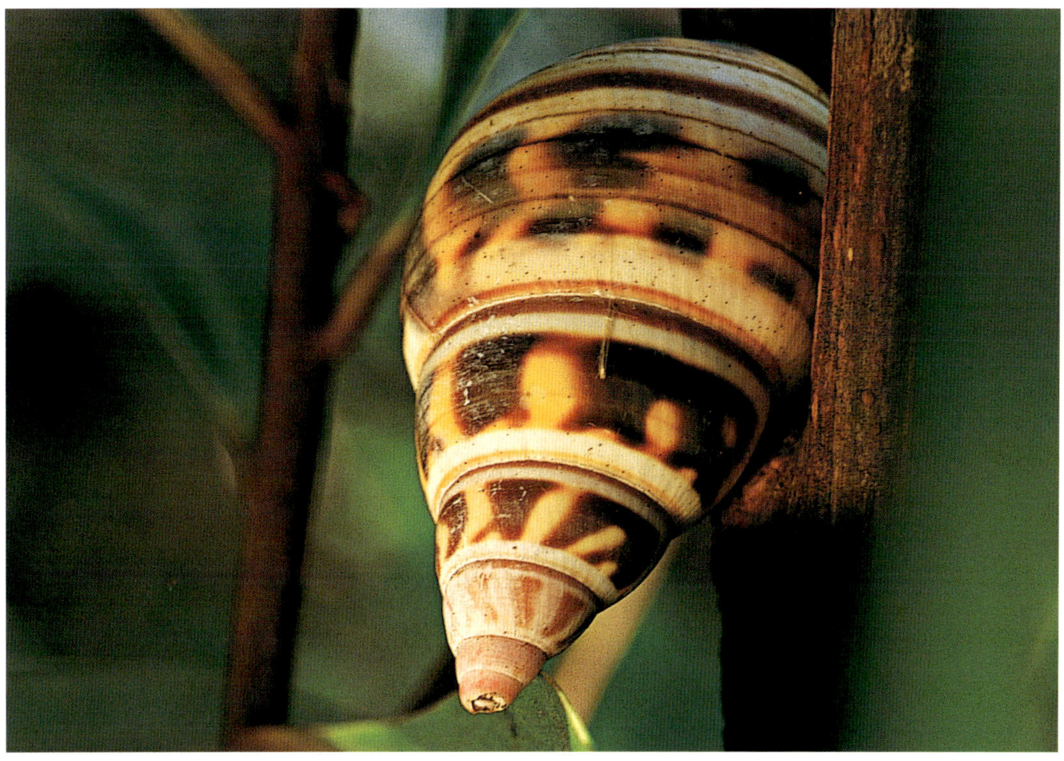

ABOVE: A Florida tree snail nestles in some branches at Everglades National Park.
SHARON GERIG/TOM STACK & ASSOCIATES

LEFT: Tricolored heron chicks survey their surroundings from a rookery nest near Kissimmee.

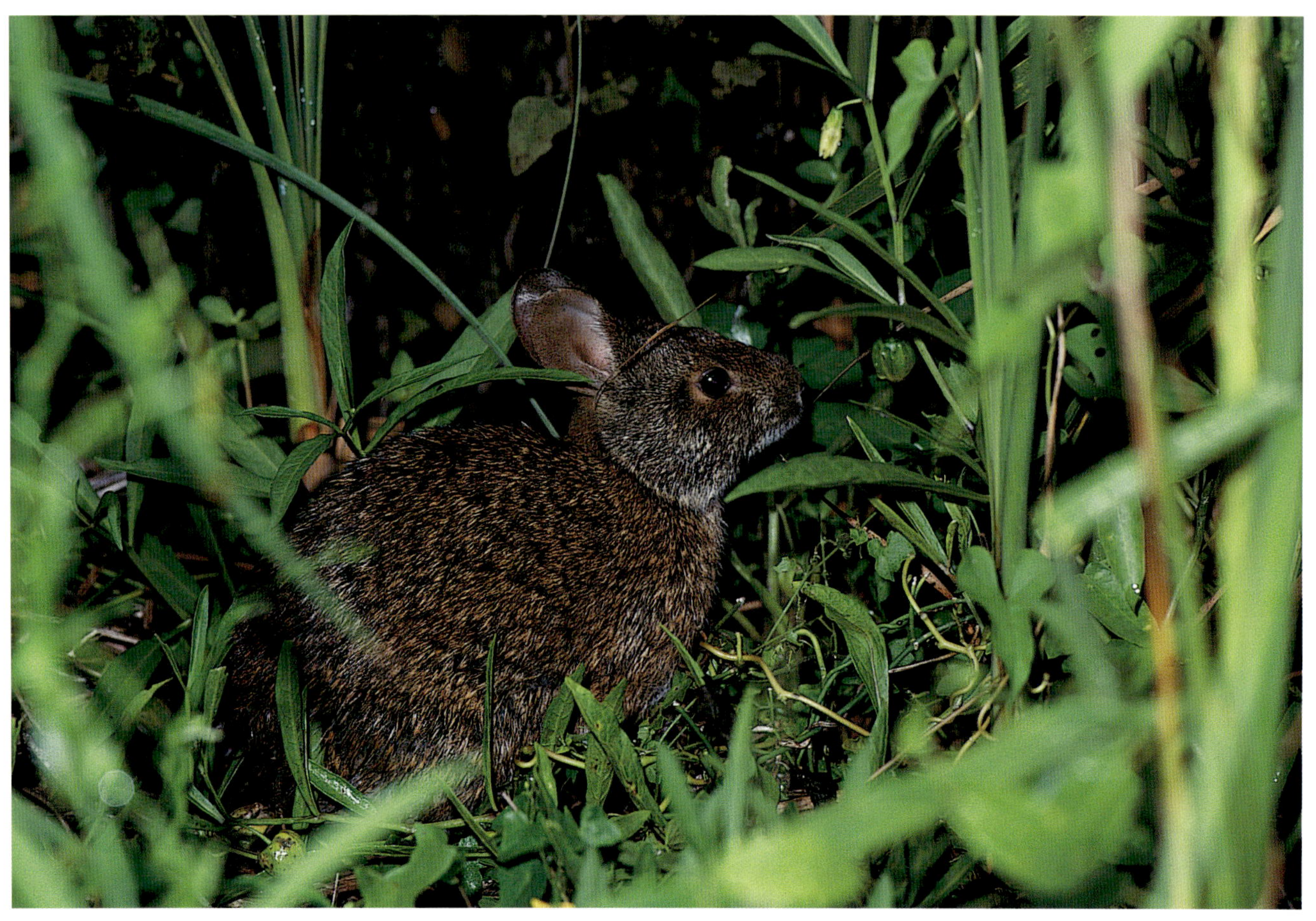

ABOVE: This marsh rabbit is hiding in dewy greenery at J. N. "Ding" Darling National Wildlife Refuge on Sanibel Island.

FACING PAGE: A red fox peers cautiously from its den.

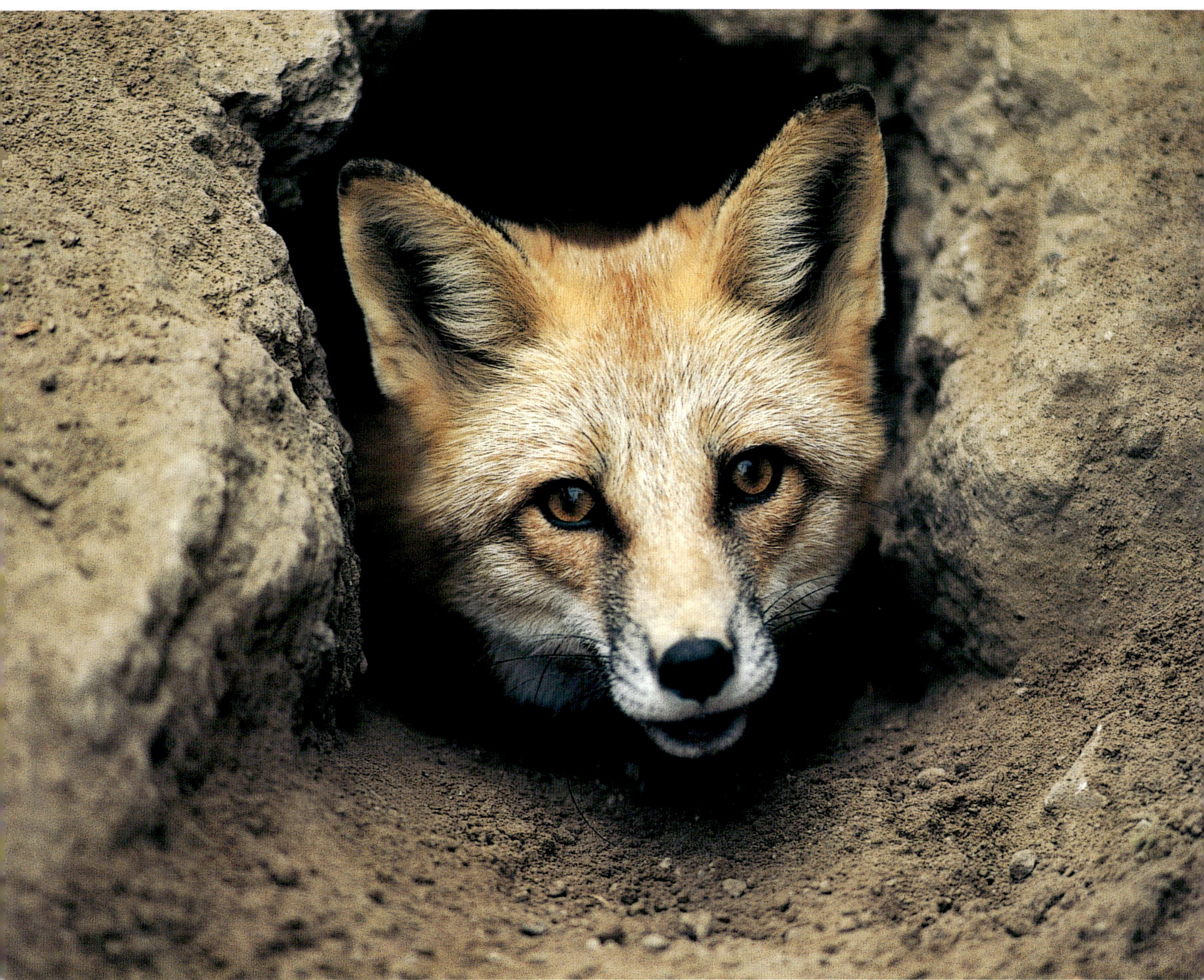

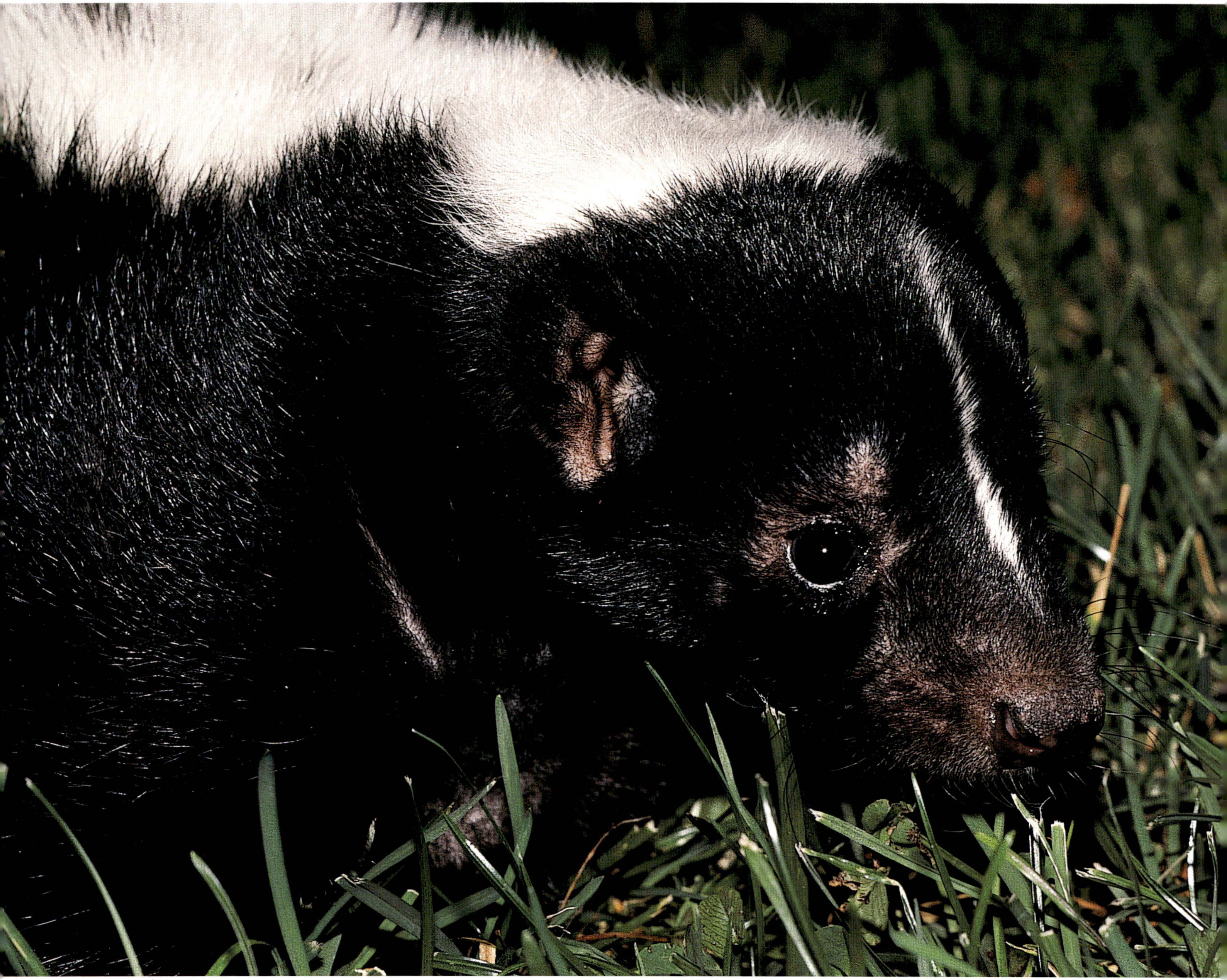

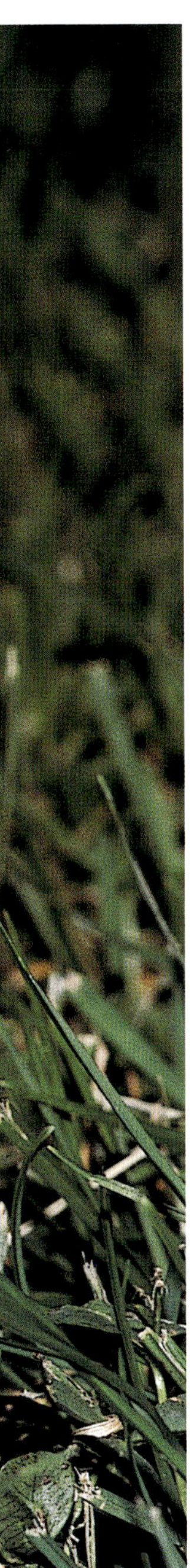

LEFT: An inquisitive striped skunk, common throughout Florida, ambles through a backyard lawn after dark.

BELOW: Wild turkeys in courtship display.
JOE MCDONALD/TOM STACK & ASSOCIATES

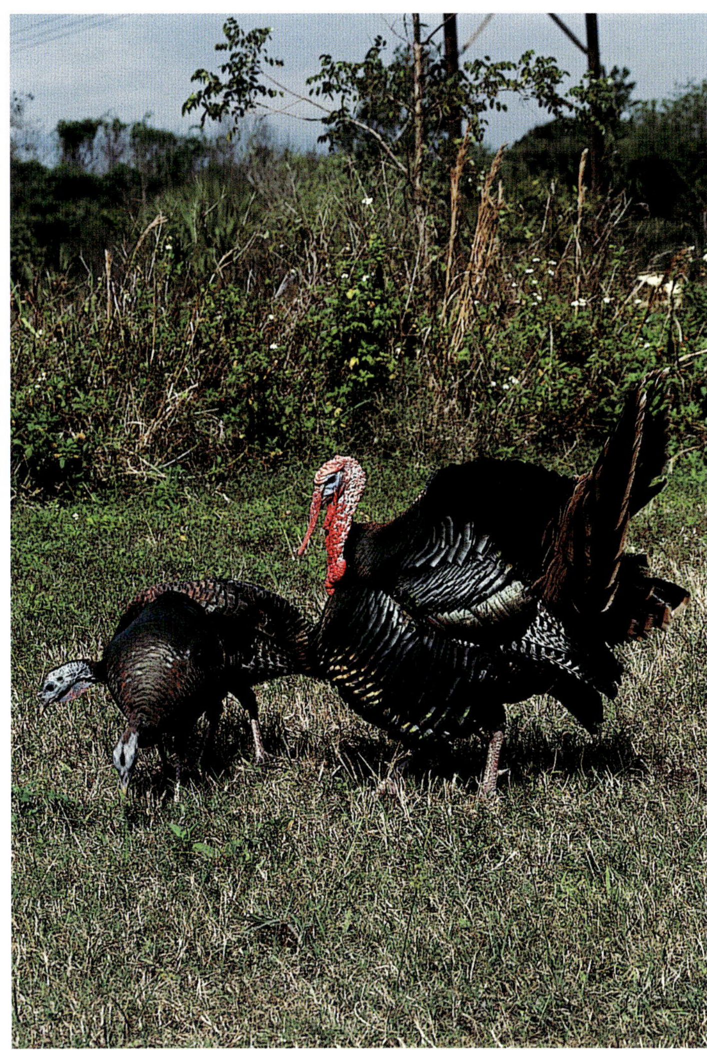

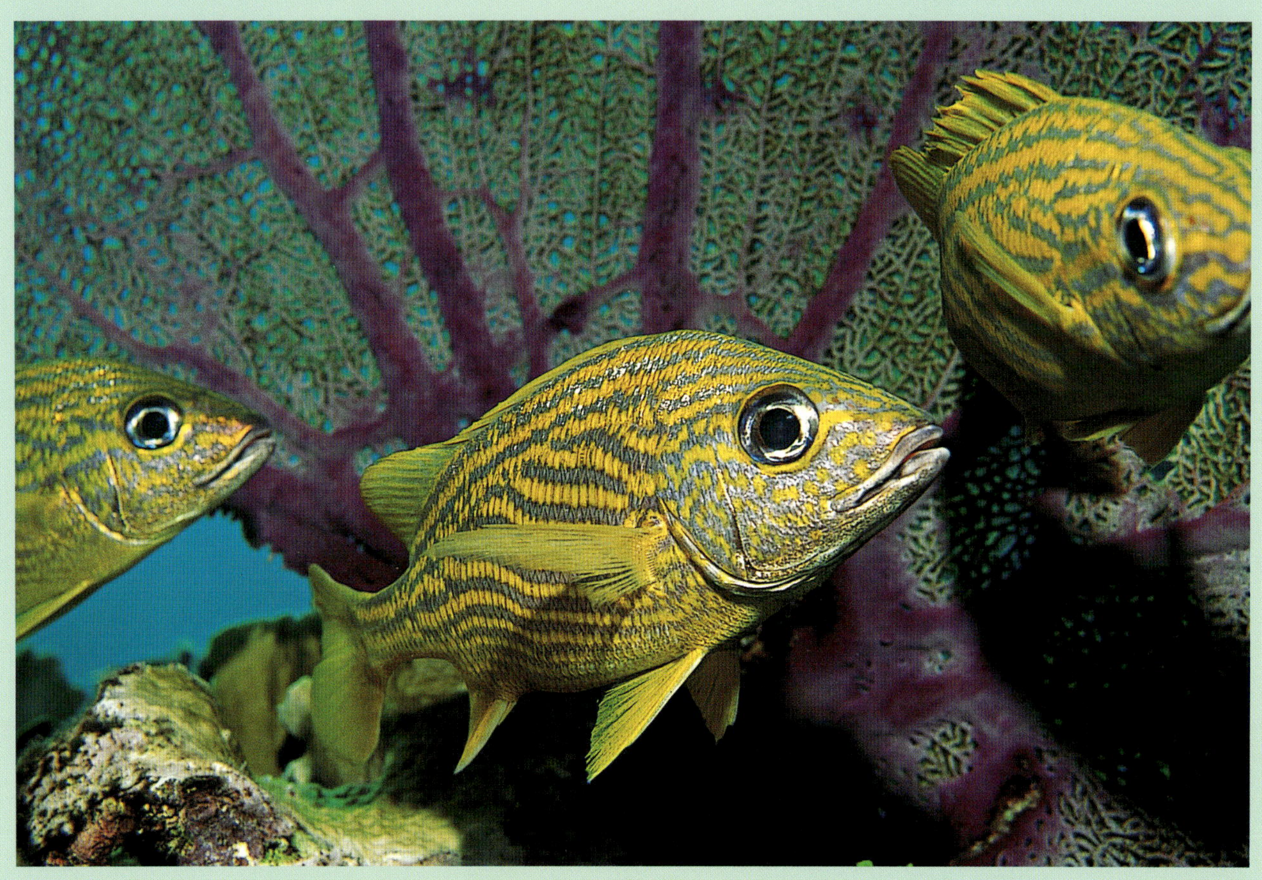

ABOVE: French grunts hover beside a sea fan in the John Pennekamp Coral Reef State Park off Key Largo.

FACING PAGE: A balloonfish peeks through branches of sea rod coral.

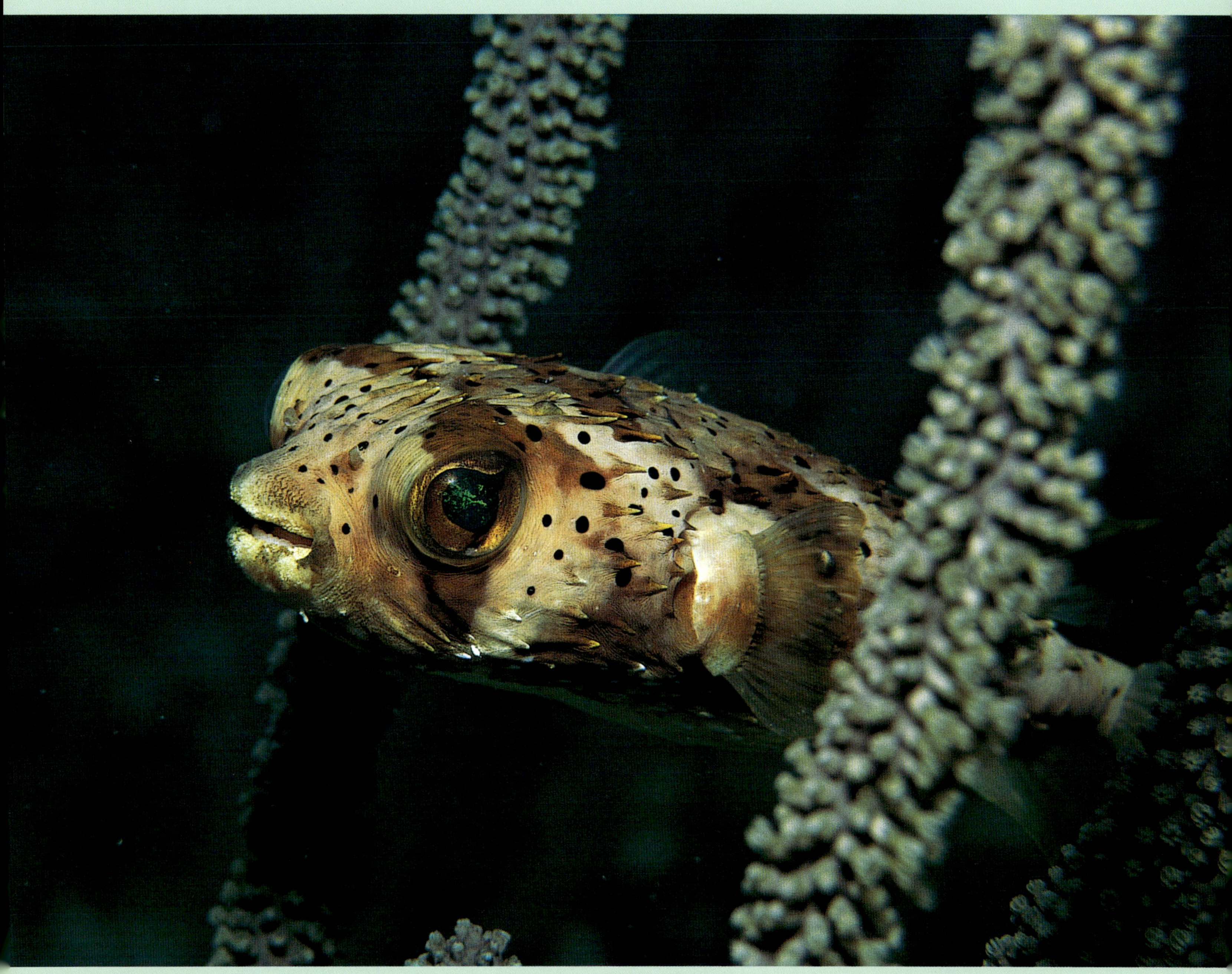

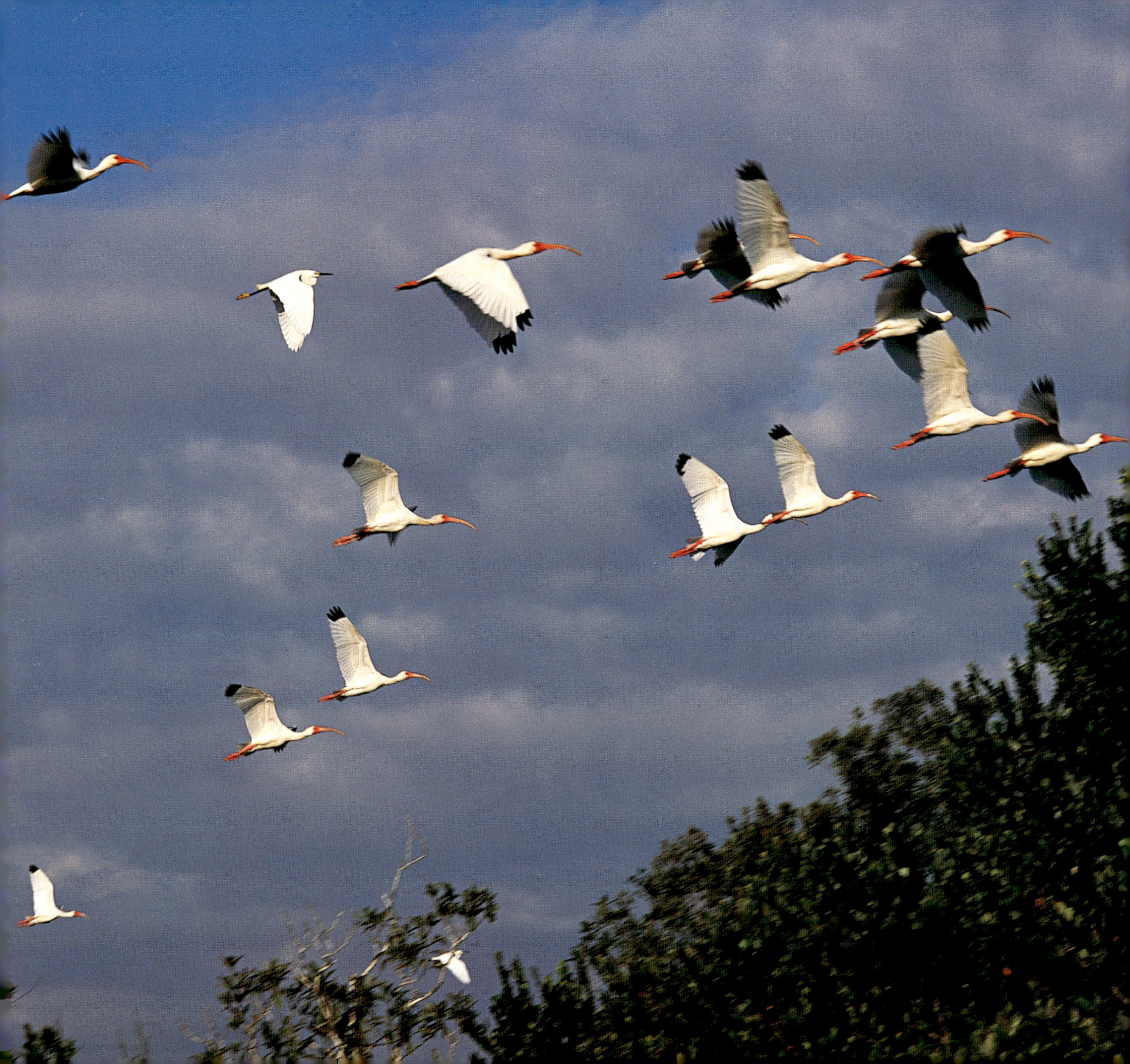

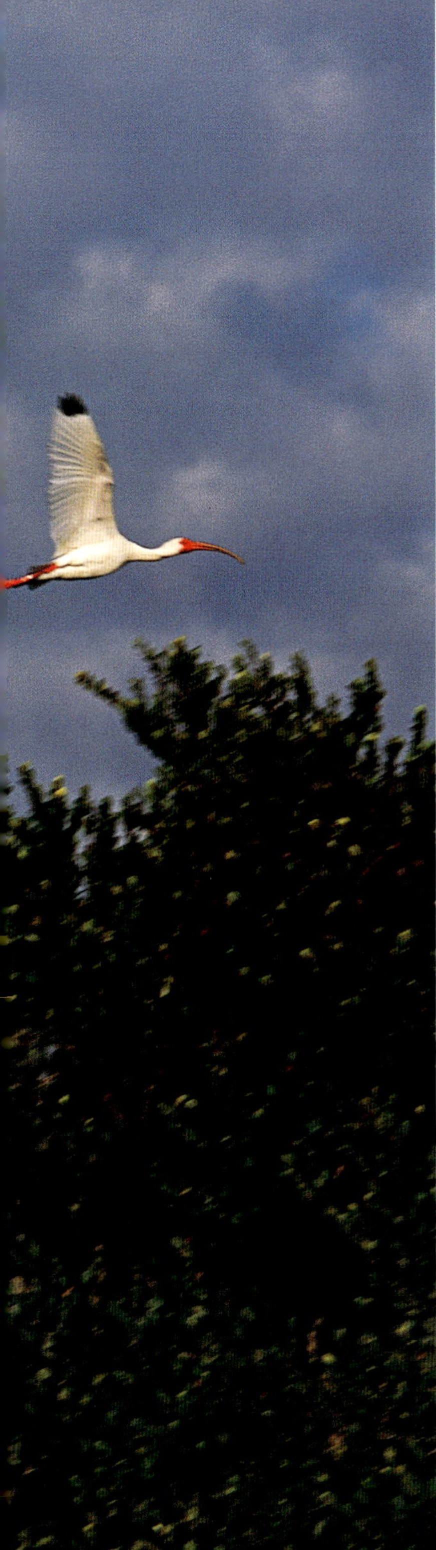

LEFT: White ibises take flight at daybreak, Shark Valley, Everglades National Park.

BELOW: A great blue heron explores the surf on Captiva Island off Florida's west coast.

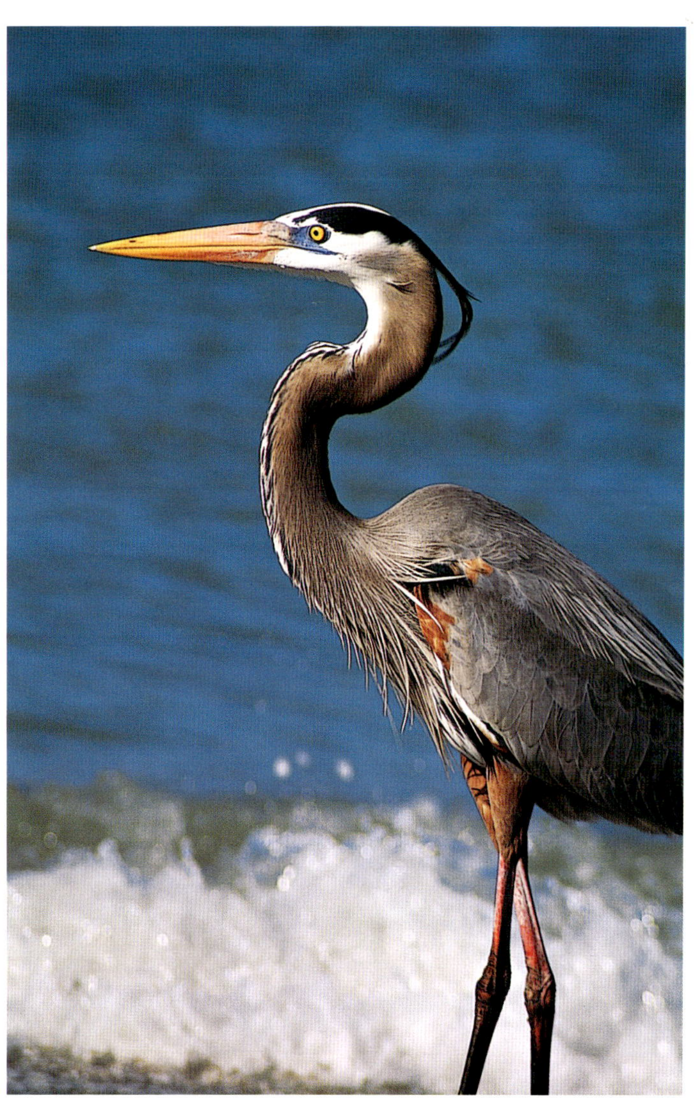

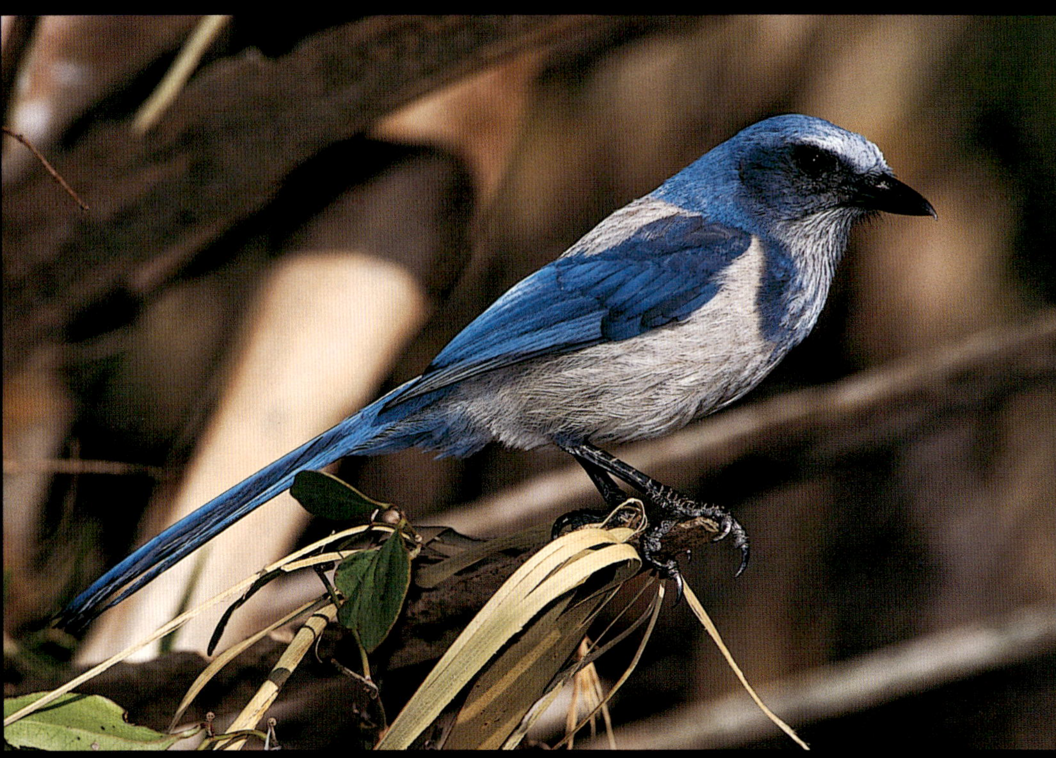

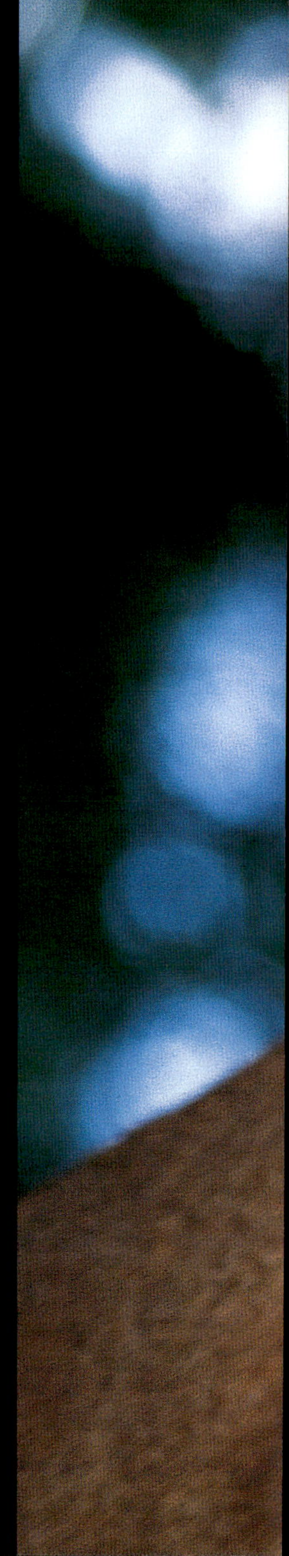

ABOVE: Inhabitants of the dry and sandy coastlines of Florida, the threatened Florida scrub jay is especially susceptible to habitat loss.
JOE MCDONALD/TOM STACK & ASSOCIATES

RIGHT: An endangered Florida panther wanders through a clearing in a hardwood hammock.

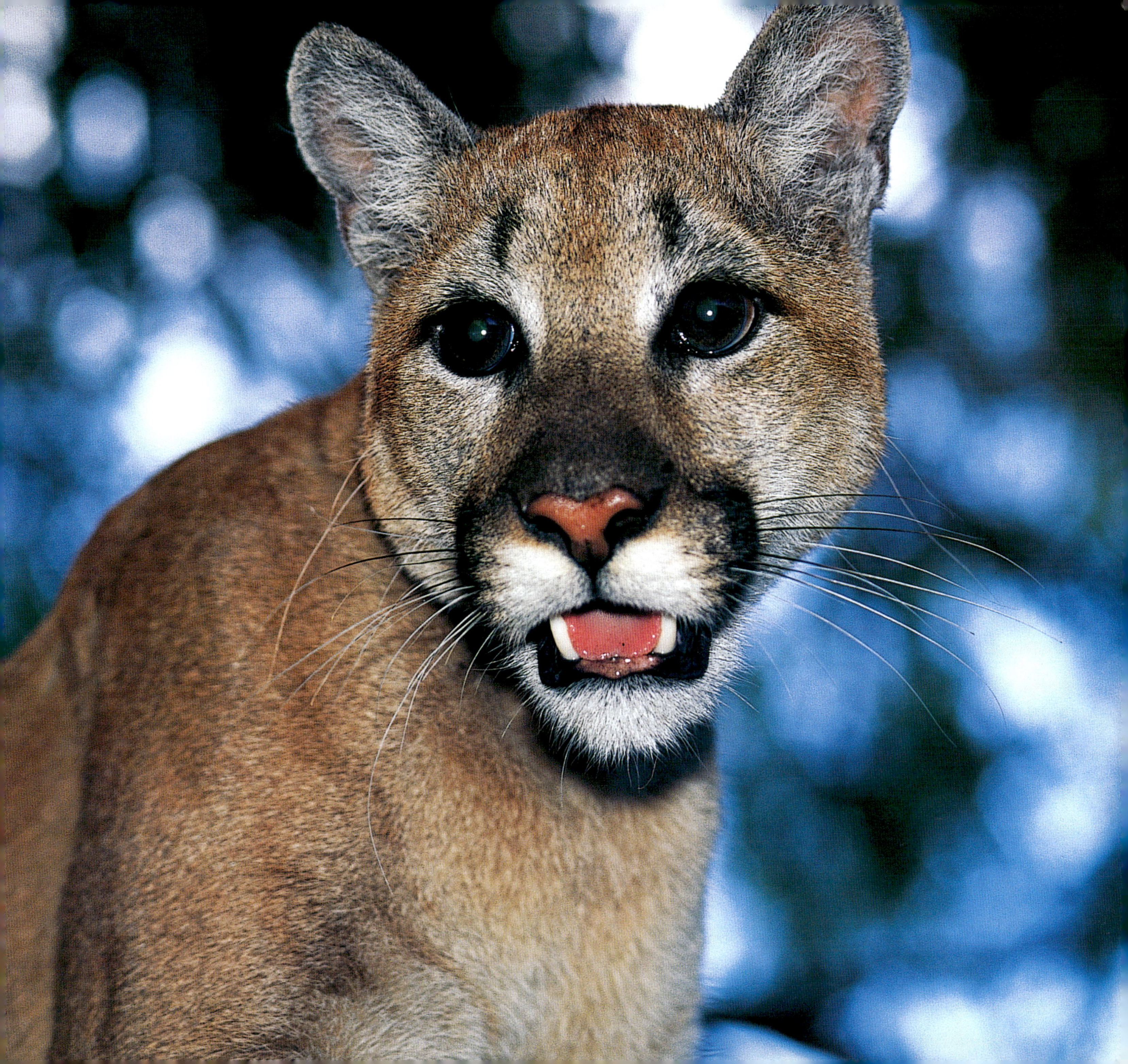

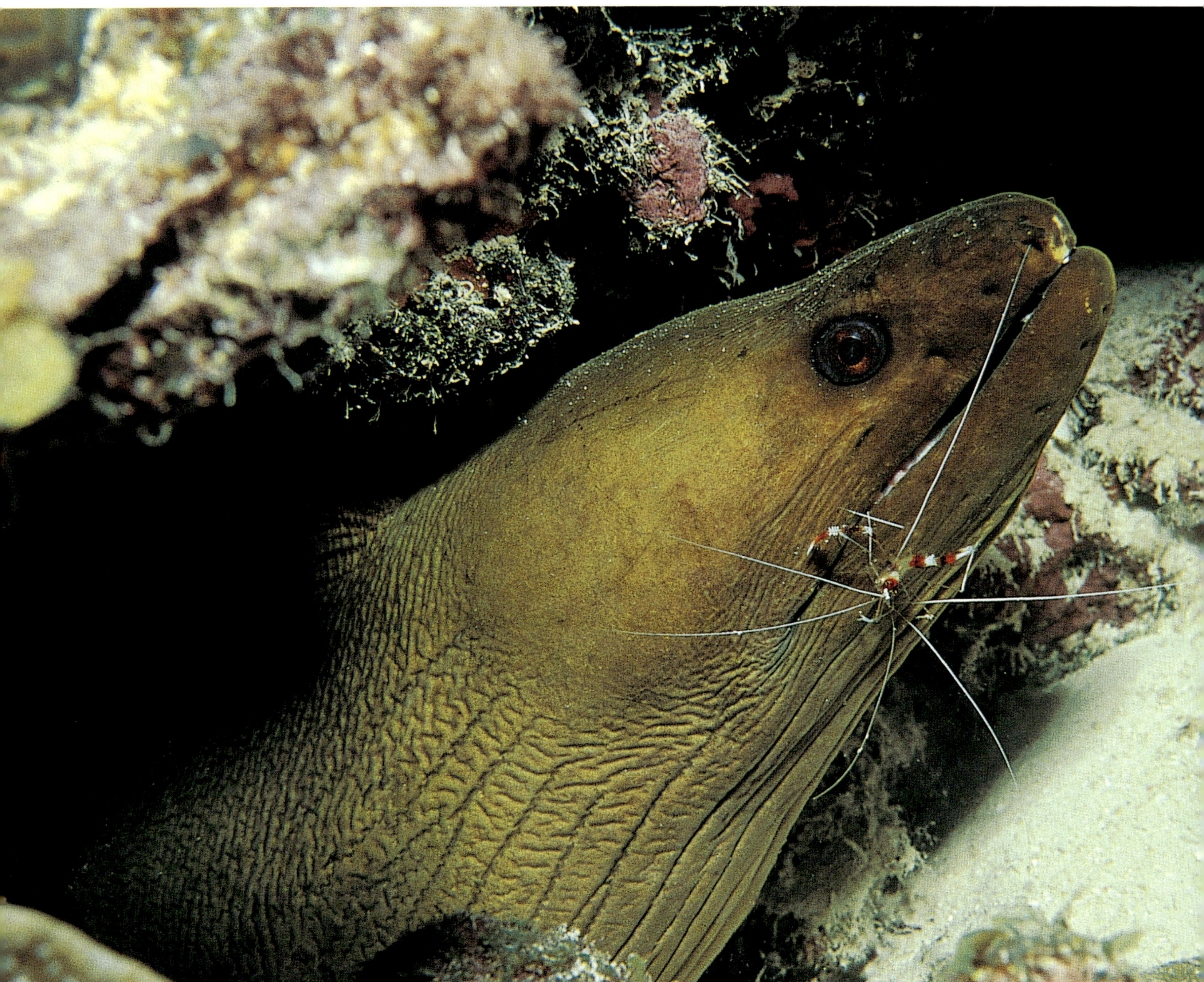

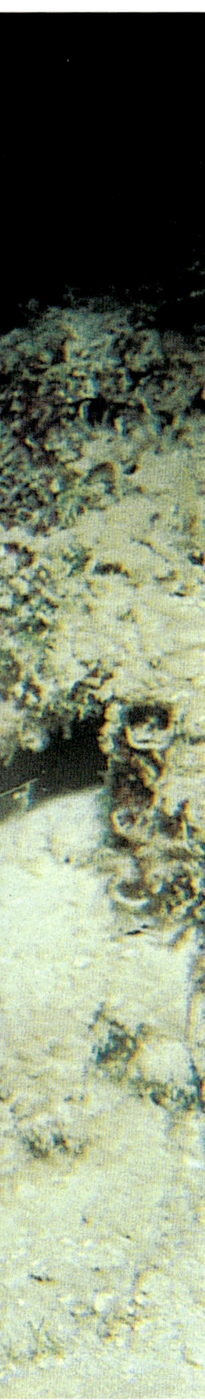

LEFT: In a display of symbiosis, a green moray eel allows itself to be cleaned by a coral cleaner shrimp.

BELOW: Hatchling loggerhead sea turtles on Juno Beach scamper for the safety of the Atlantic Ocean.

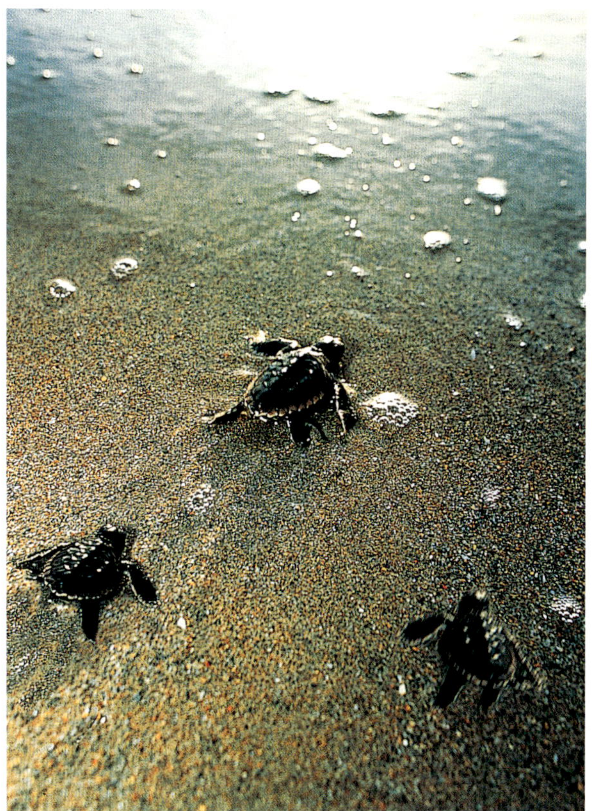

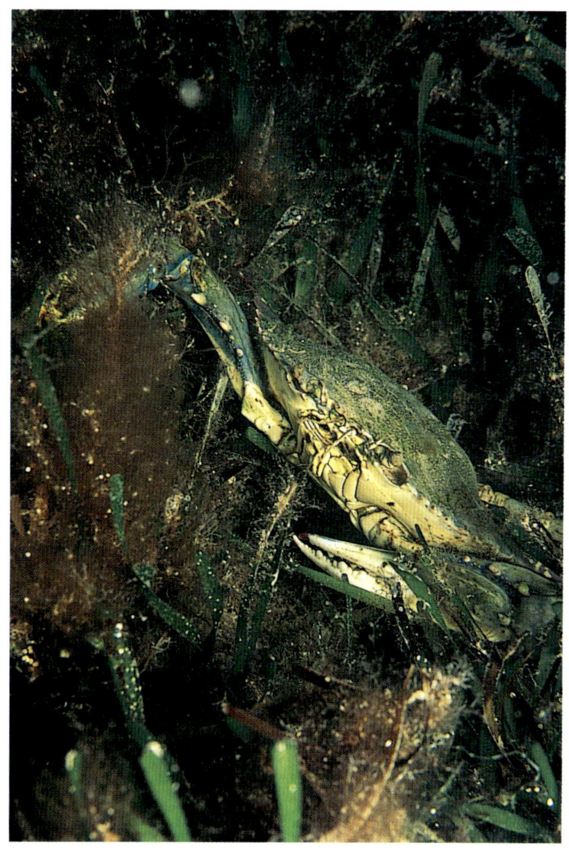

ABOVE: A blue crab attempts to hide in the Florida Bay sea grass.

RIGHT: The historic, unpaved Loop Road through Big Cypress National Preserve offers wonderful opportunities to view river otters and other wildlife.

FAR RIGHT: A southern stingray makes its way over the sandy bottom of the Florida Keys National Marine Sanctuary.

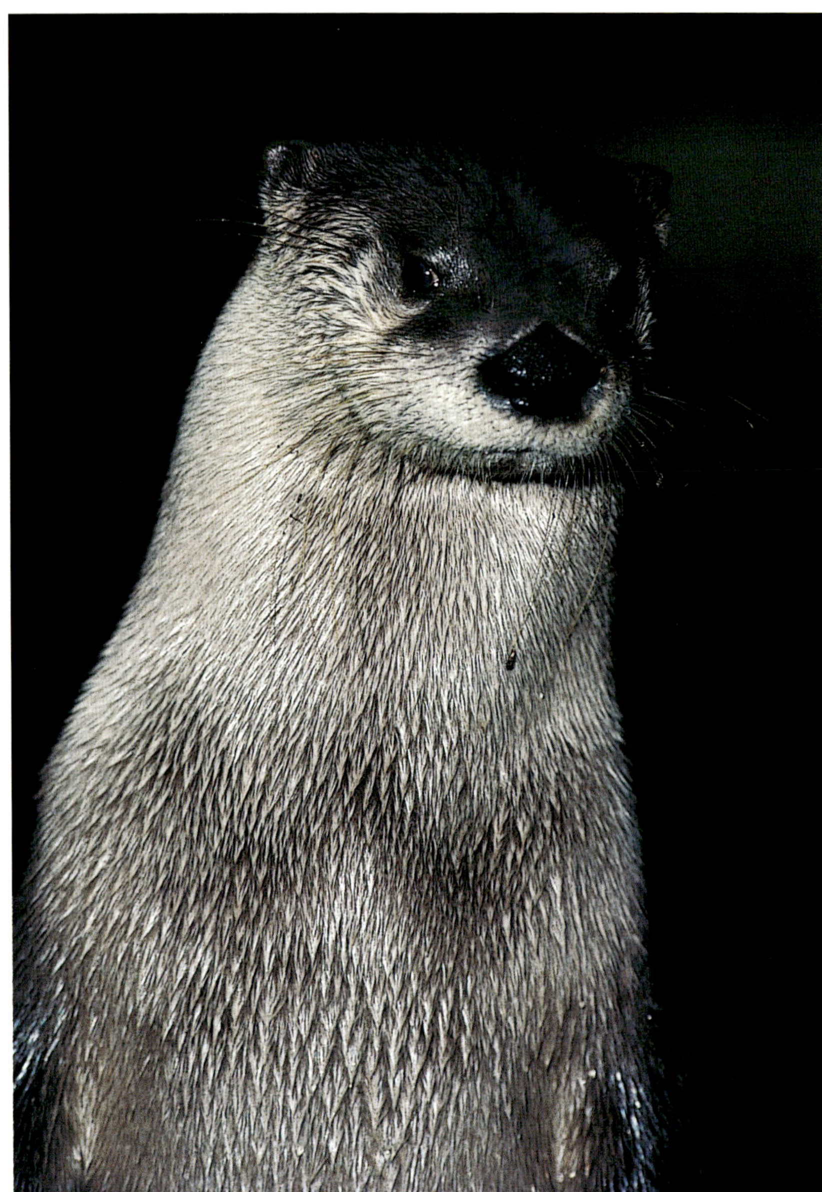

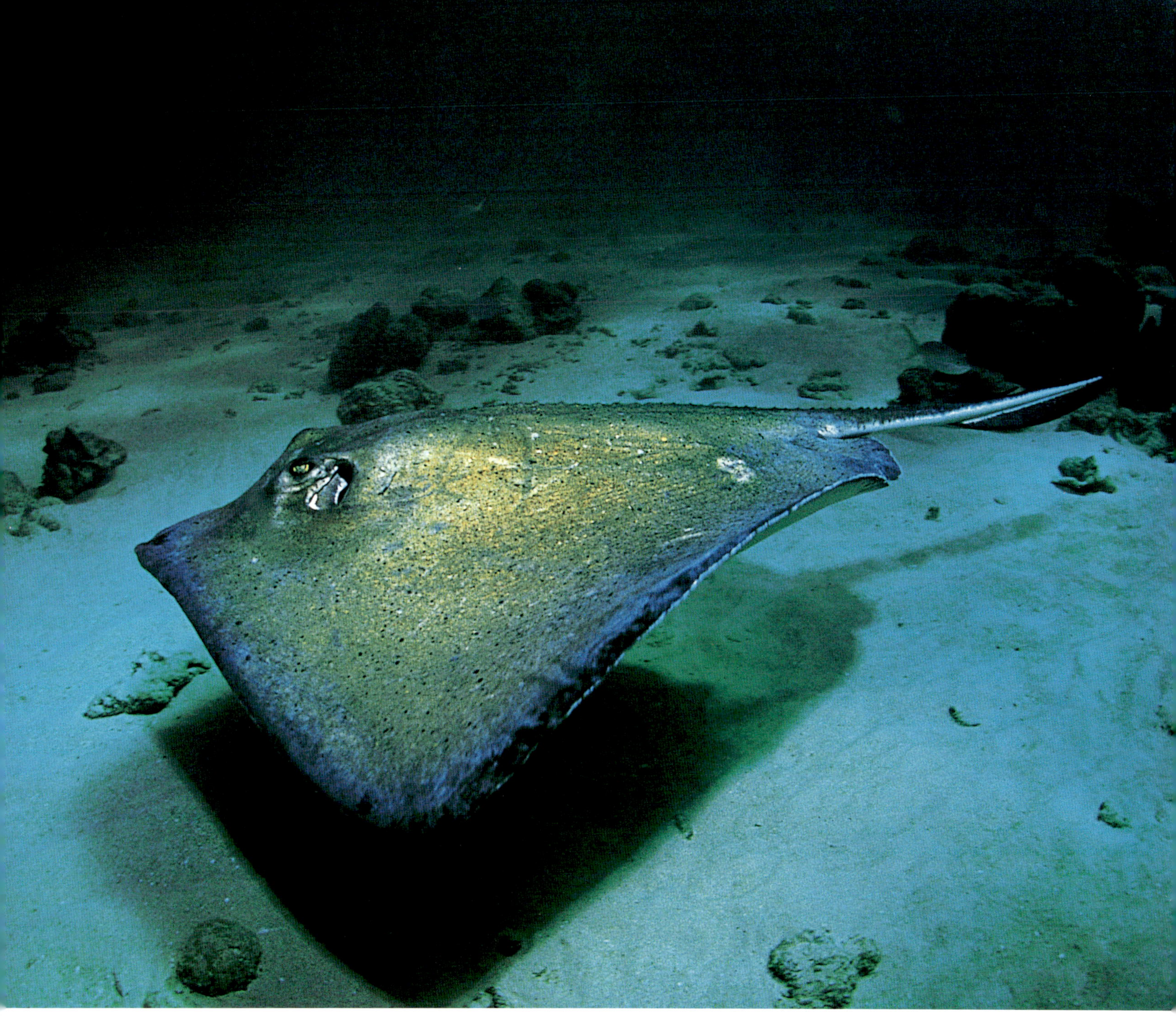

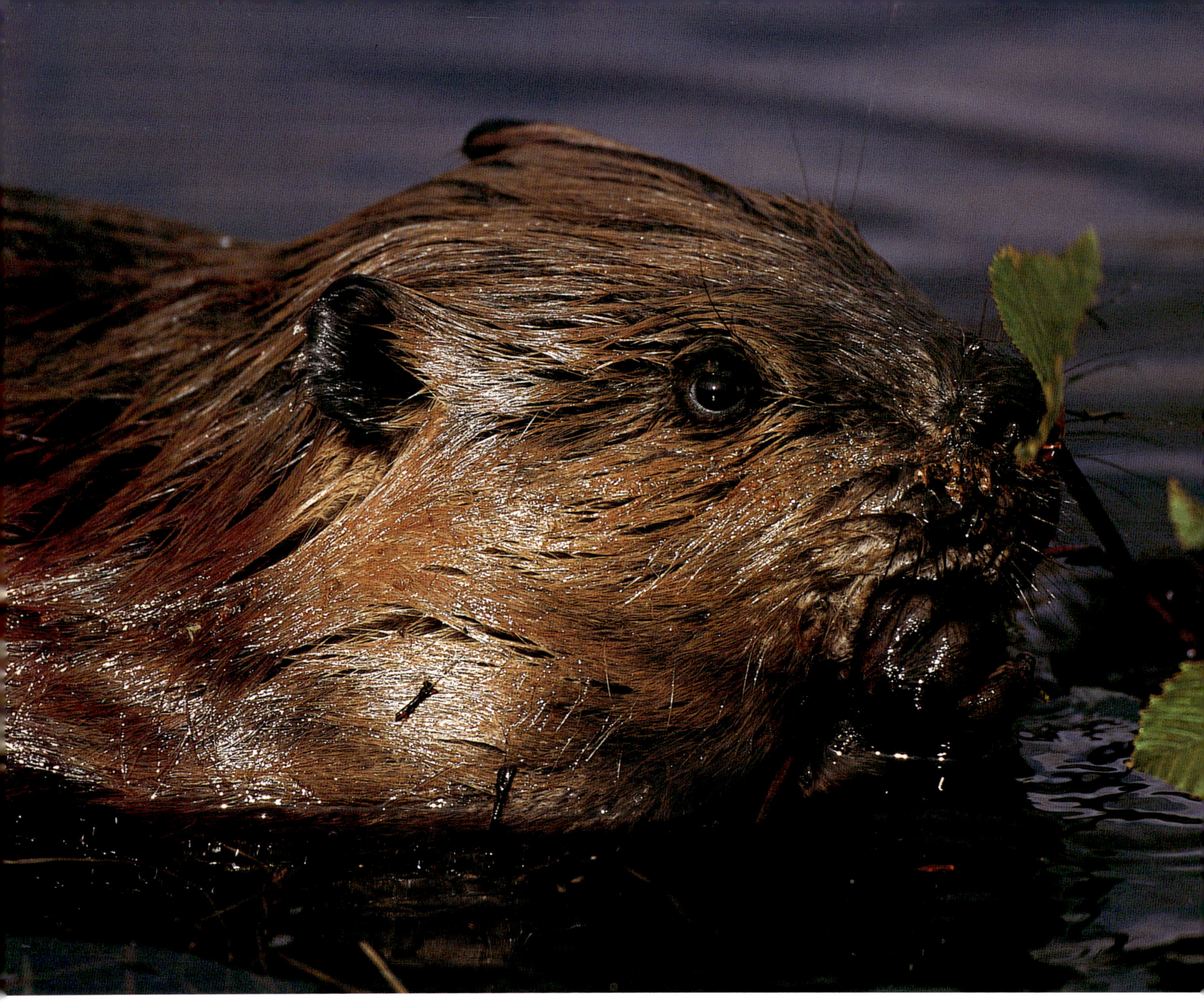

Beavers can be observed building their dams in northern Florida. THOMAS KITCHIN/TOM STACK & ASSOCIATES

Green sea turtles come ashore to lay their eggs in early summer.

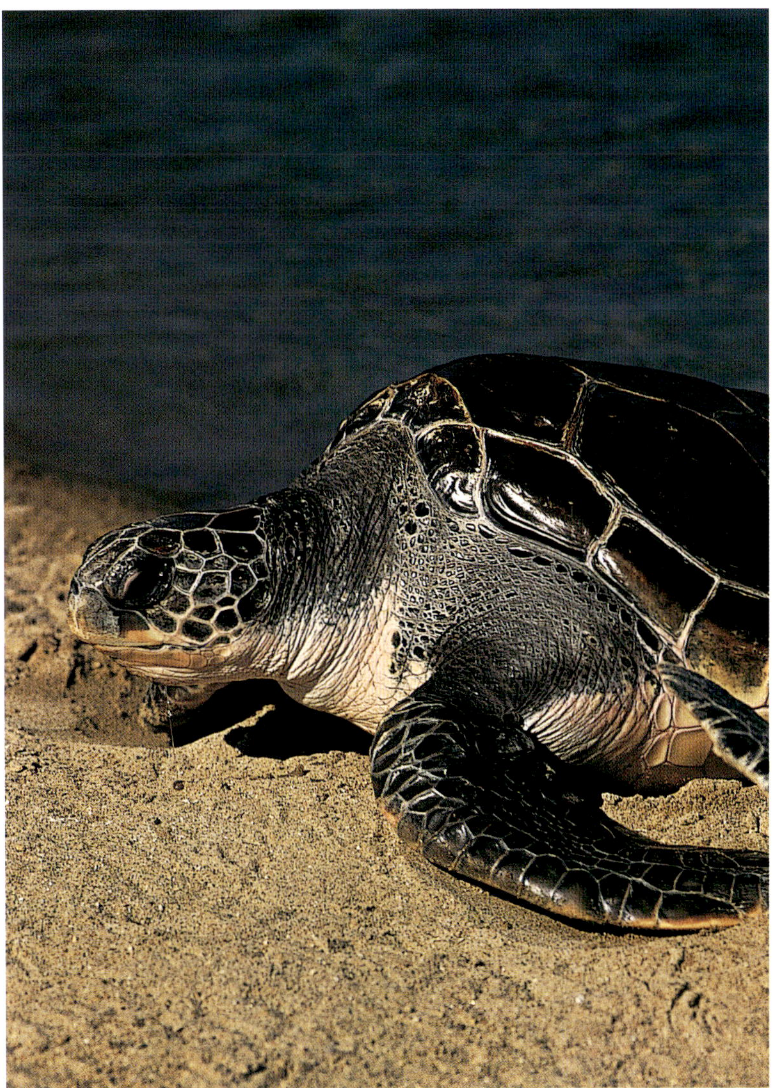

RIGHT: Brown pelicans are commonly seen around Florida's waterfronts and marinas.

FAR RIGHT: Young American alligators congregate in an "alligator hole" during the dry season. If a drought persists, the remaining water supply in the hole lures fish and birds to the alligators.

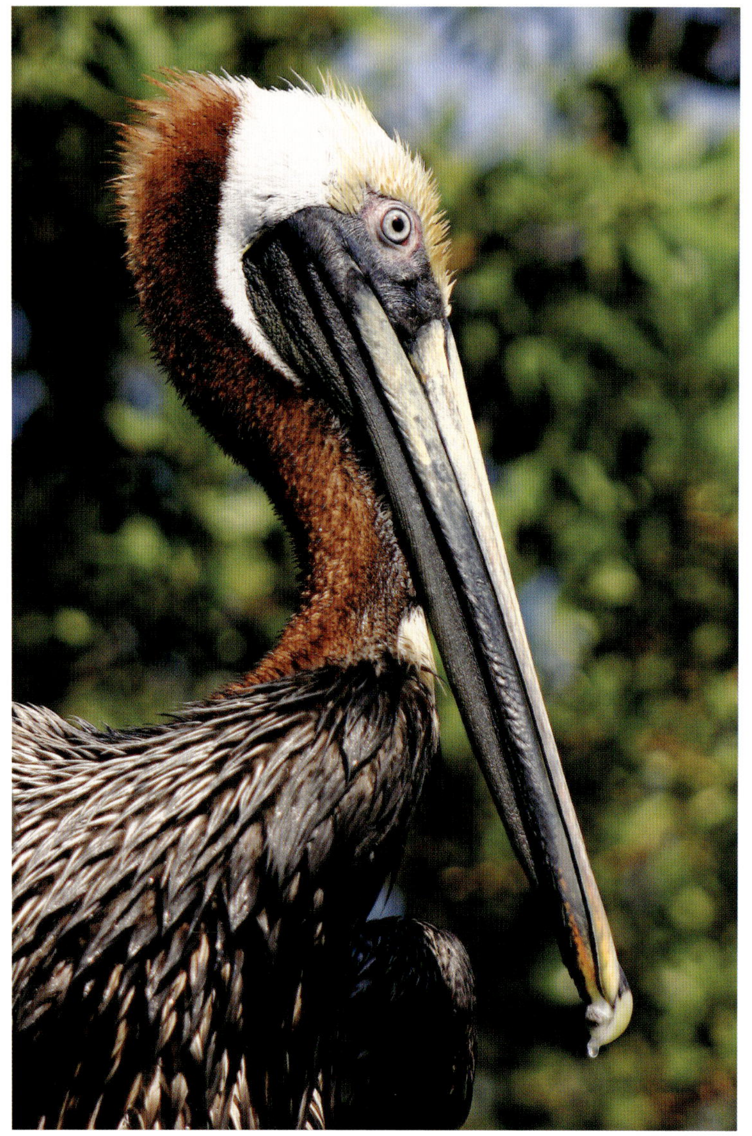

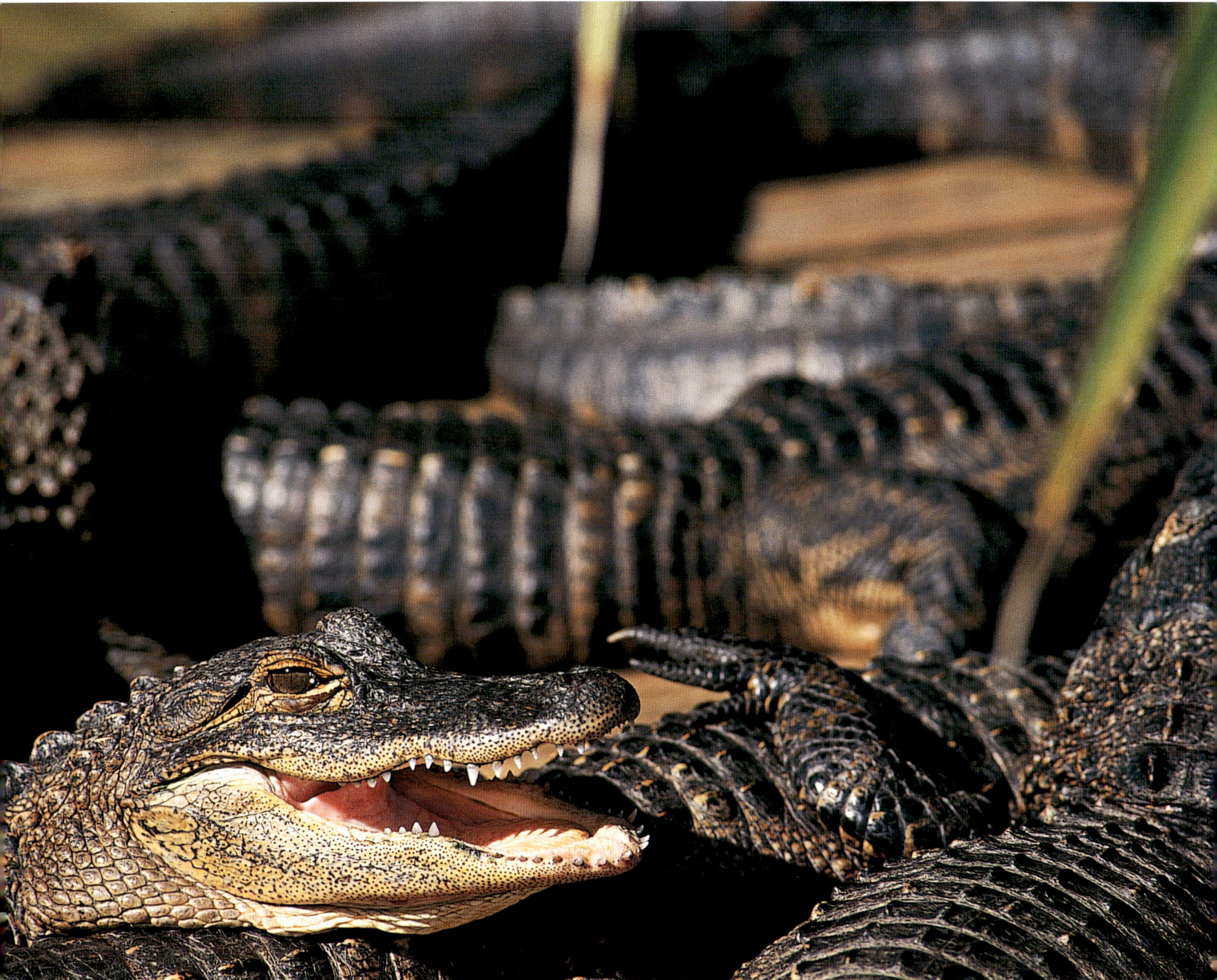

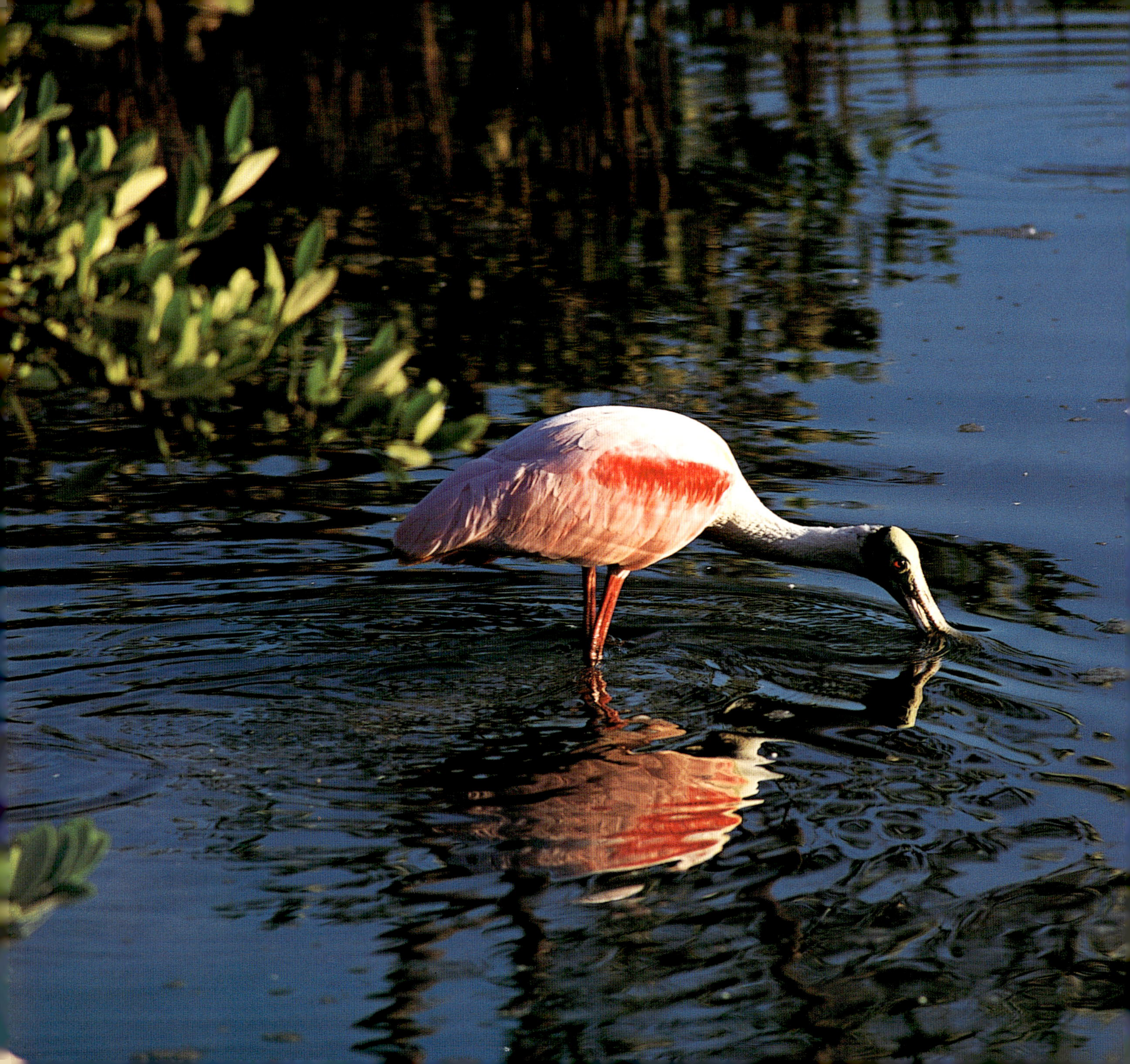

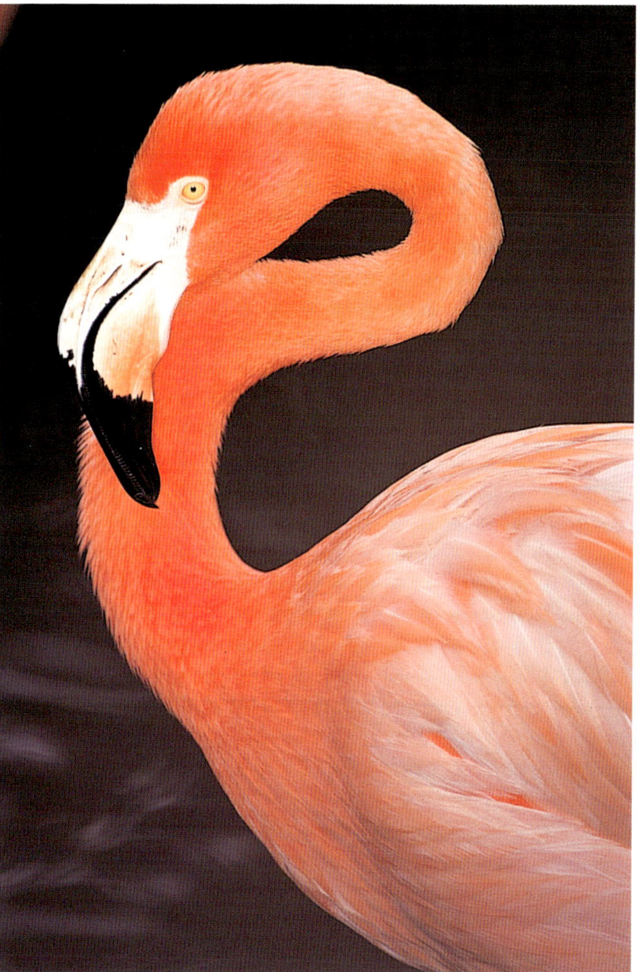

ABOVE: A greater flamingo strikes a majestic pose.

LEFT: Creating a brilliant reflection in the late afternoon light, a roseate spoonbill feeds in the shallow waters of Florida Bay, Everglades National Park.

FACING PAGE: Flying fish are amazing to see as they leap from the ocean's surface and glide over the water, utilizing their large, specialized pectoral fins.

BELOW: An endangered hawksbill sea turtle cruises through the waters of the Florida Keys National Marine Sanctuary off Tavernier.

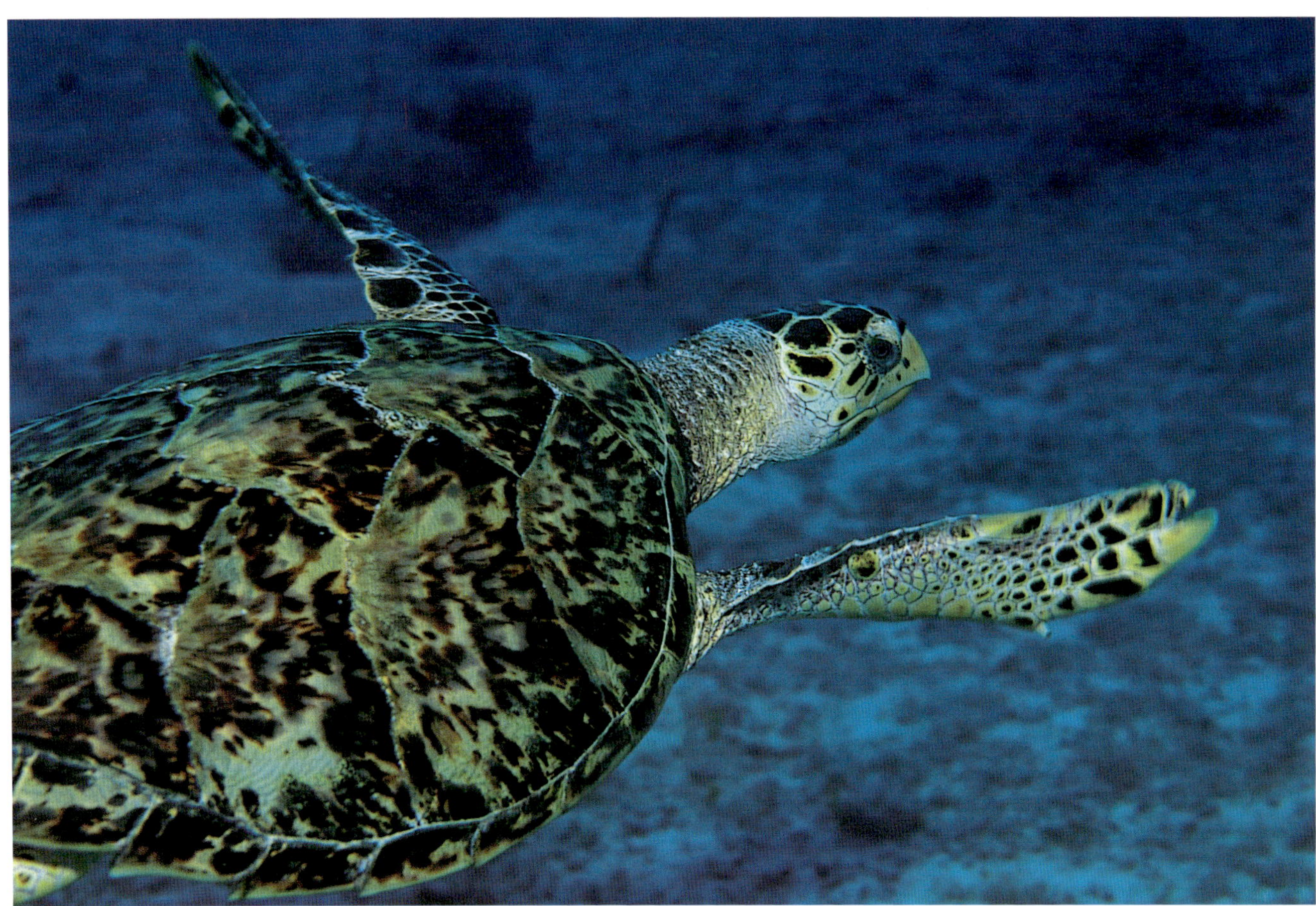

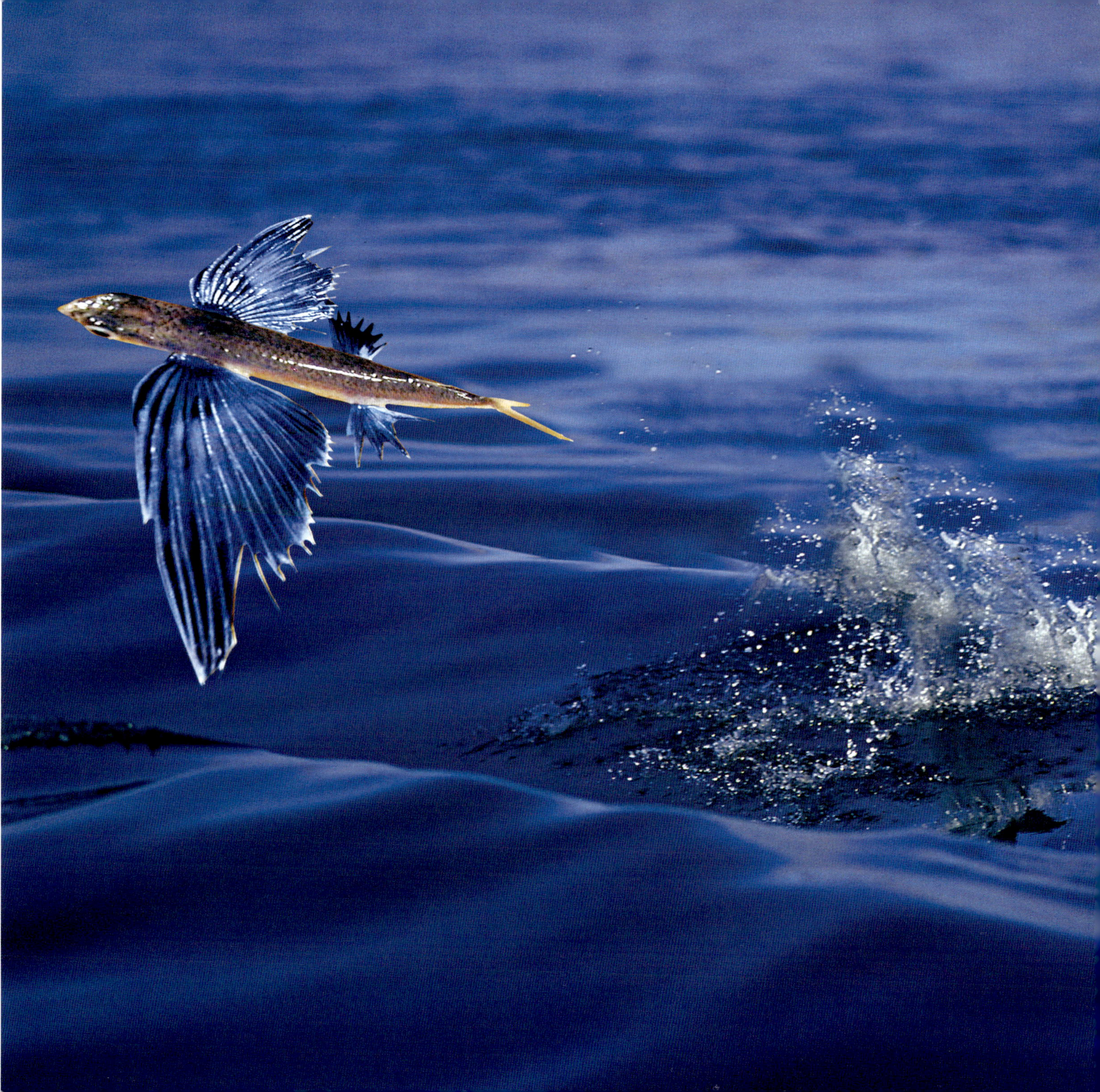

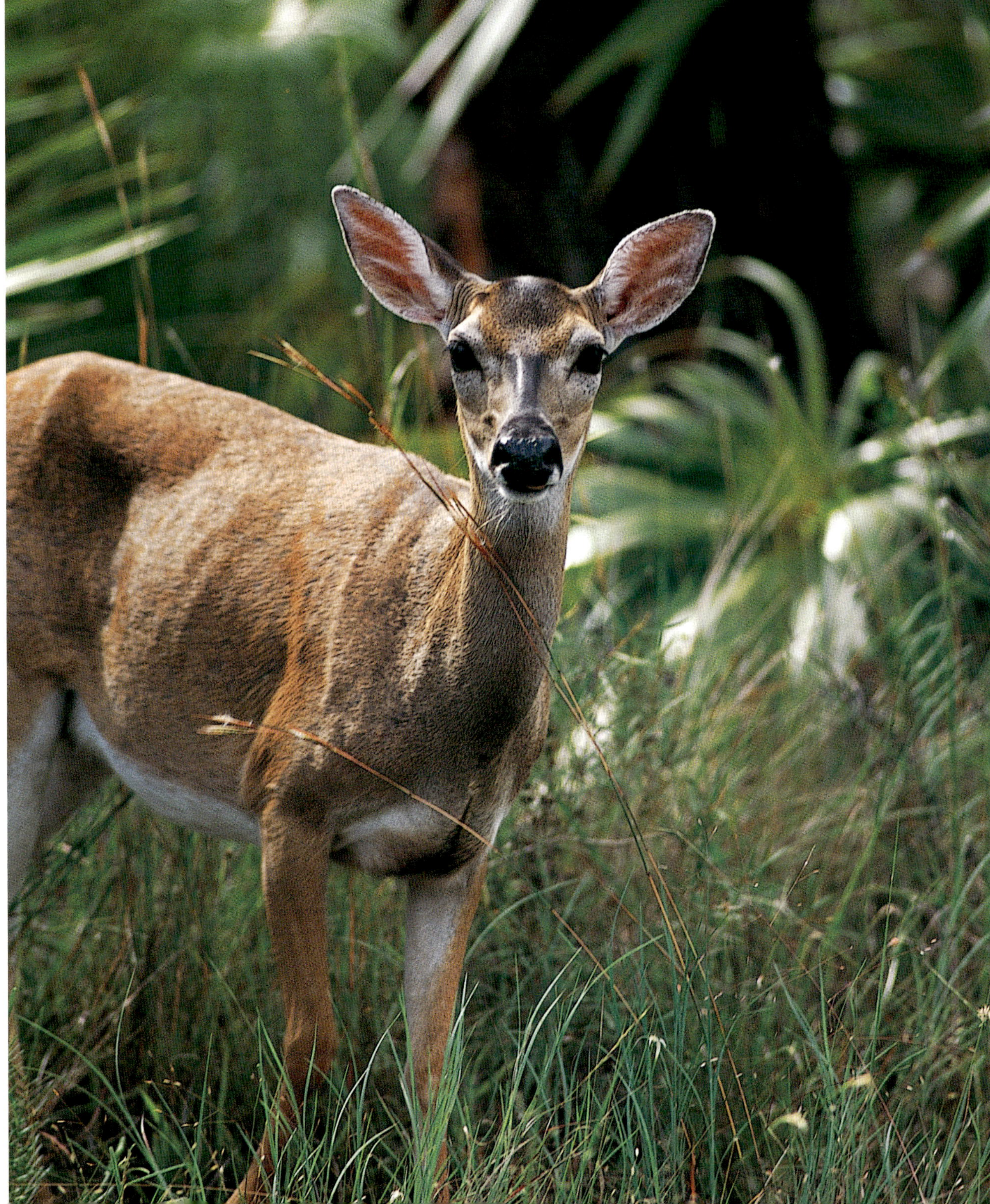

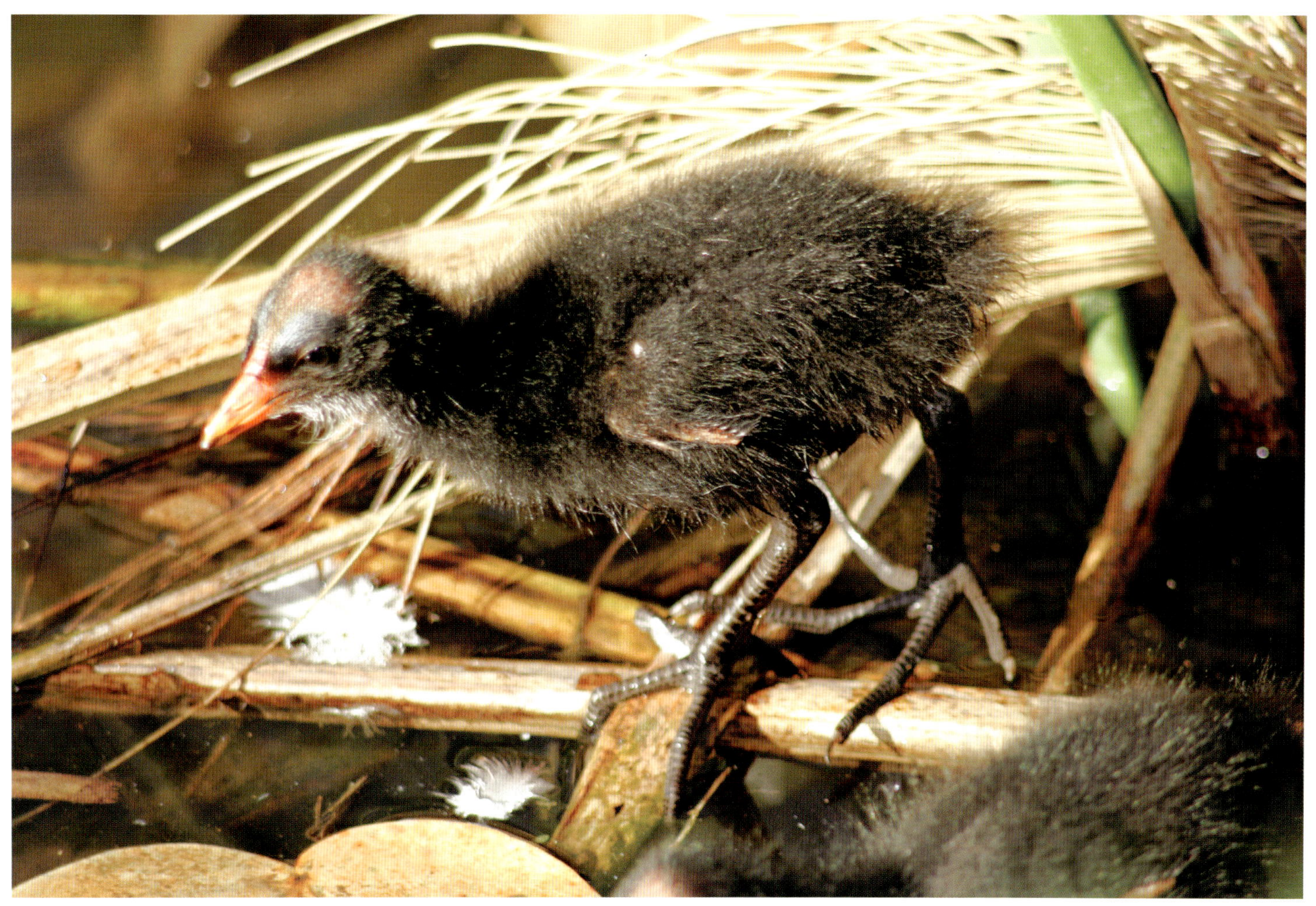

ABOVE: A common moorhen chick strides gingerly on marsh reeds in Kissimmee.

FACING PAGE: The diminutive key deer is an endangered species that can be viewed in the wild at the National Key Deer Refuge on Big Pine Key.

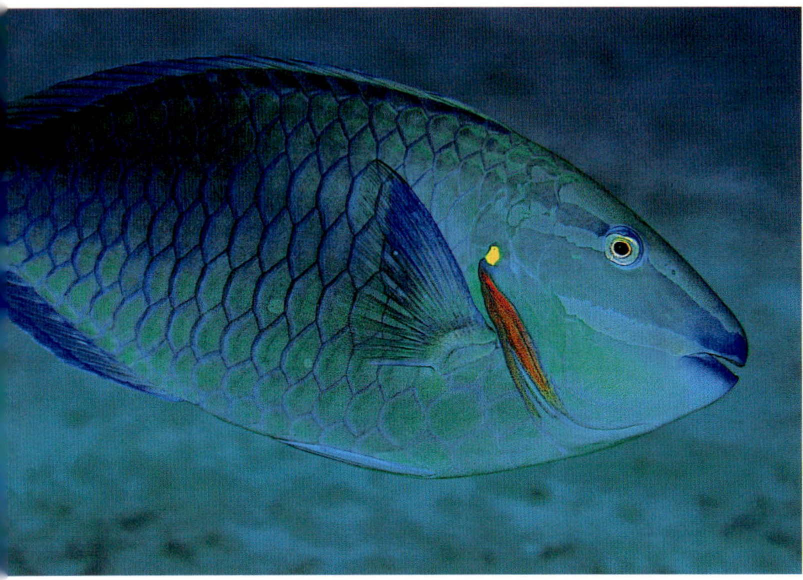

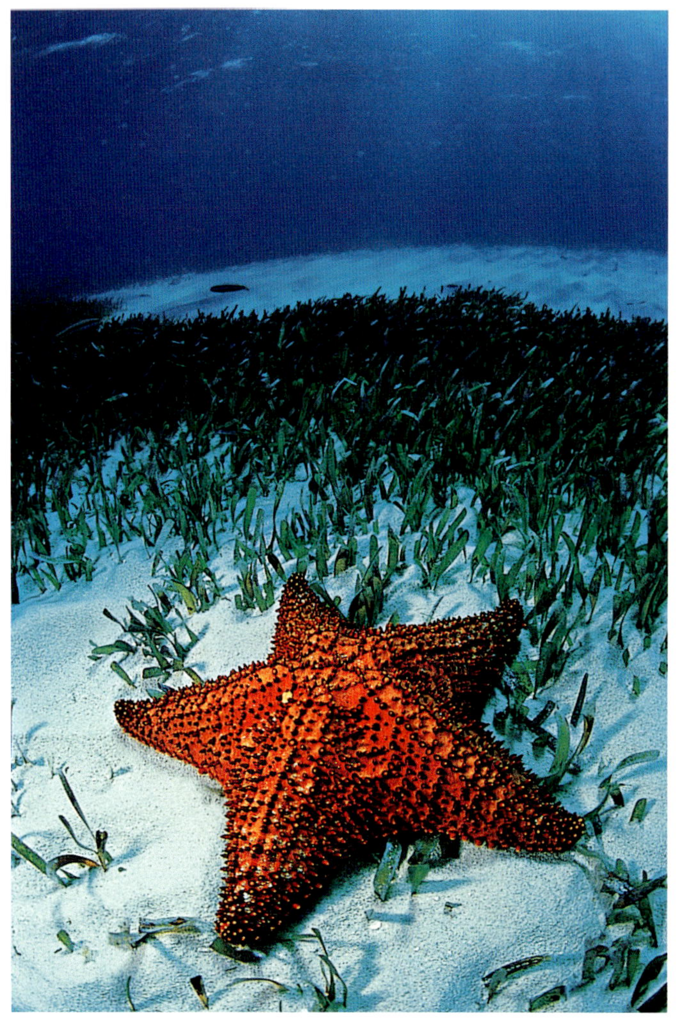

ABOVE: Stoplight parrotfish exhibit a distinguishing yellow spot at the top of their gill cover.

RIGHT: A cushion sea star moves slowly through a patch of turtle grass in the clear shallows off Islamorada.

FACING PAGE: The goliath grouper, a protected species, is impressive in both size and attitude.

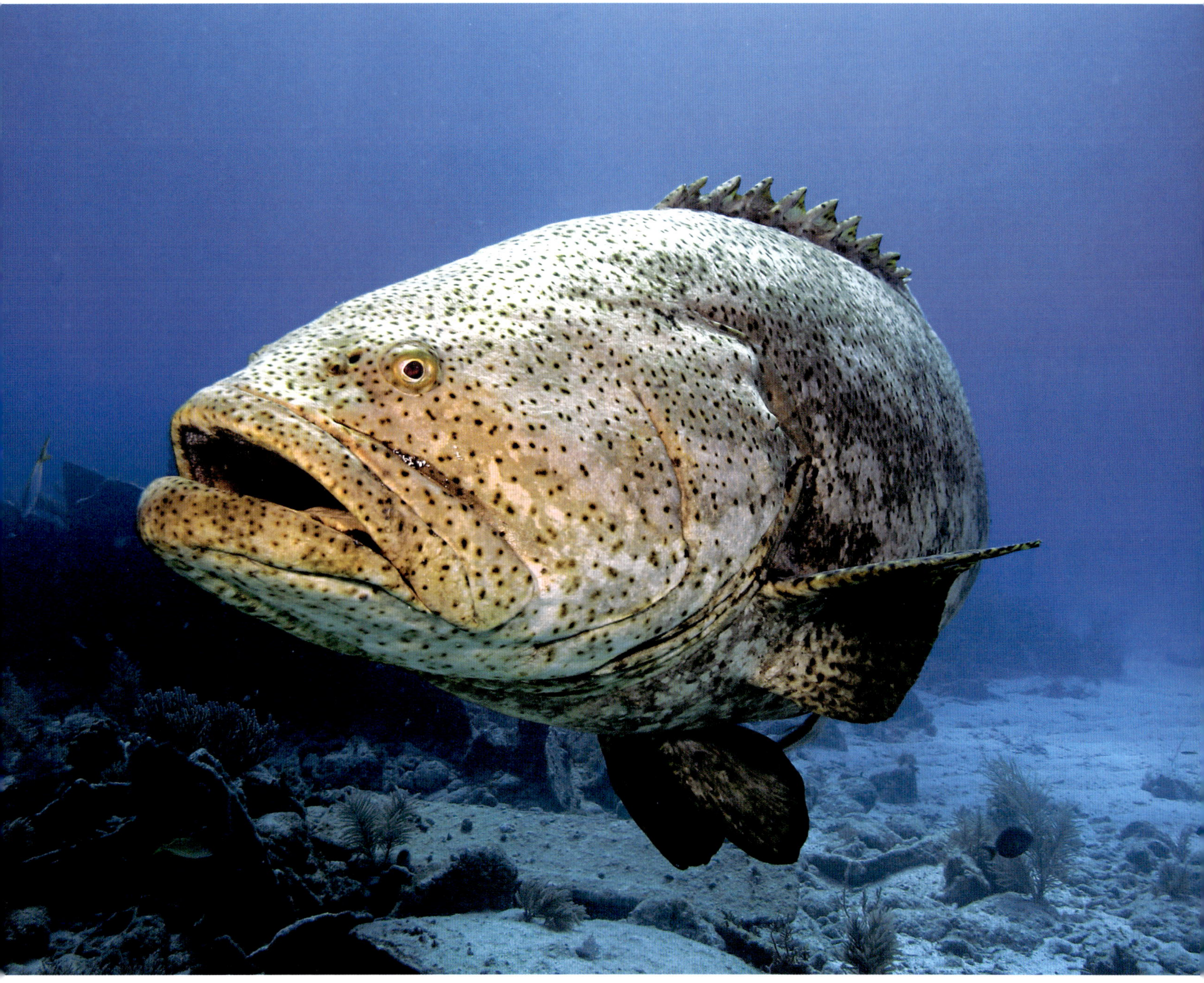

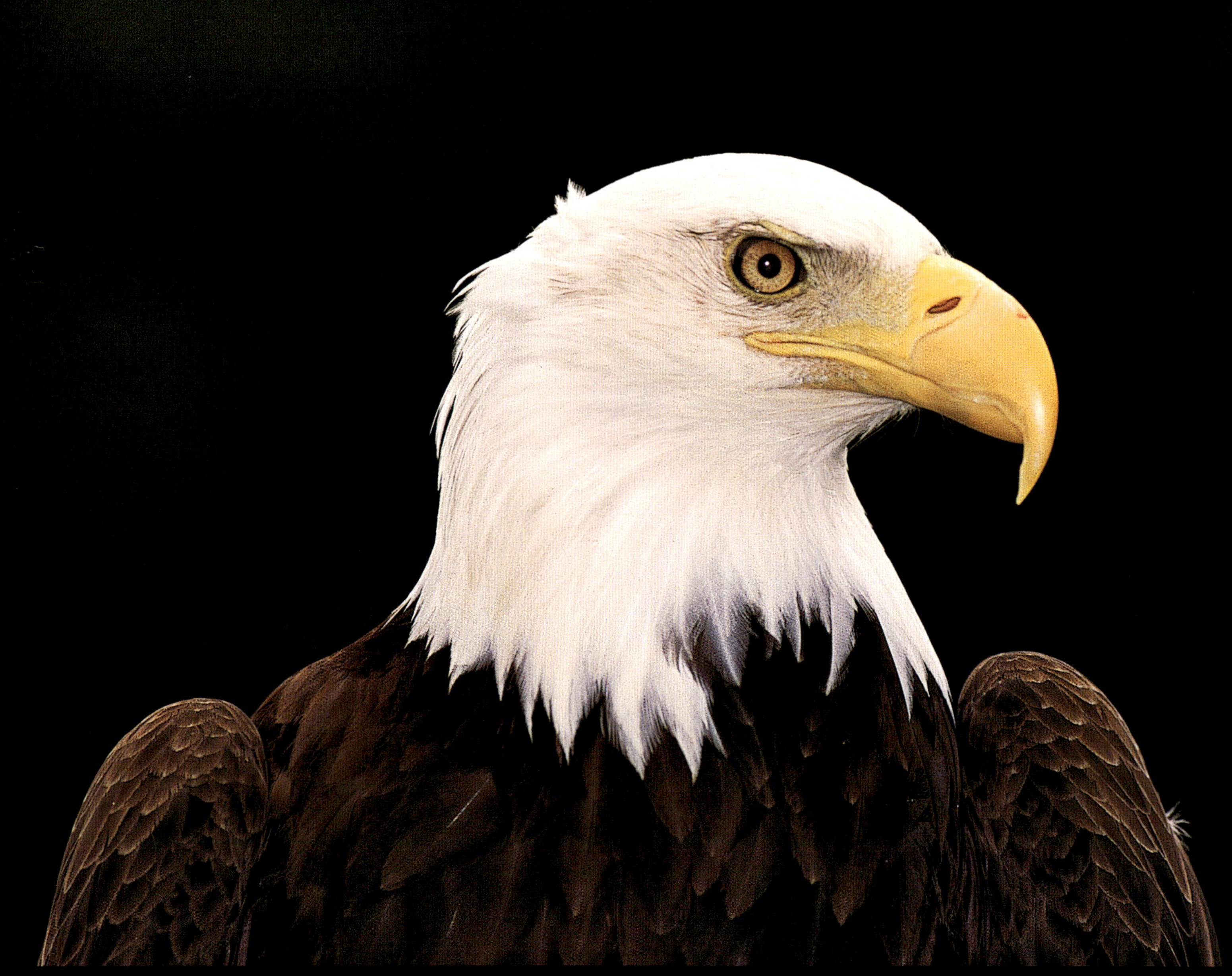

Florida is home of the largest breeding population of bald eagles of any southeastern state.

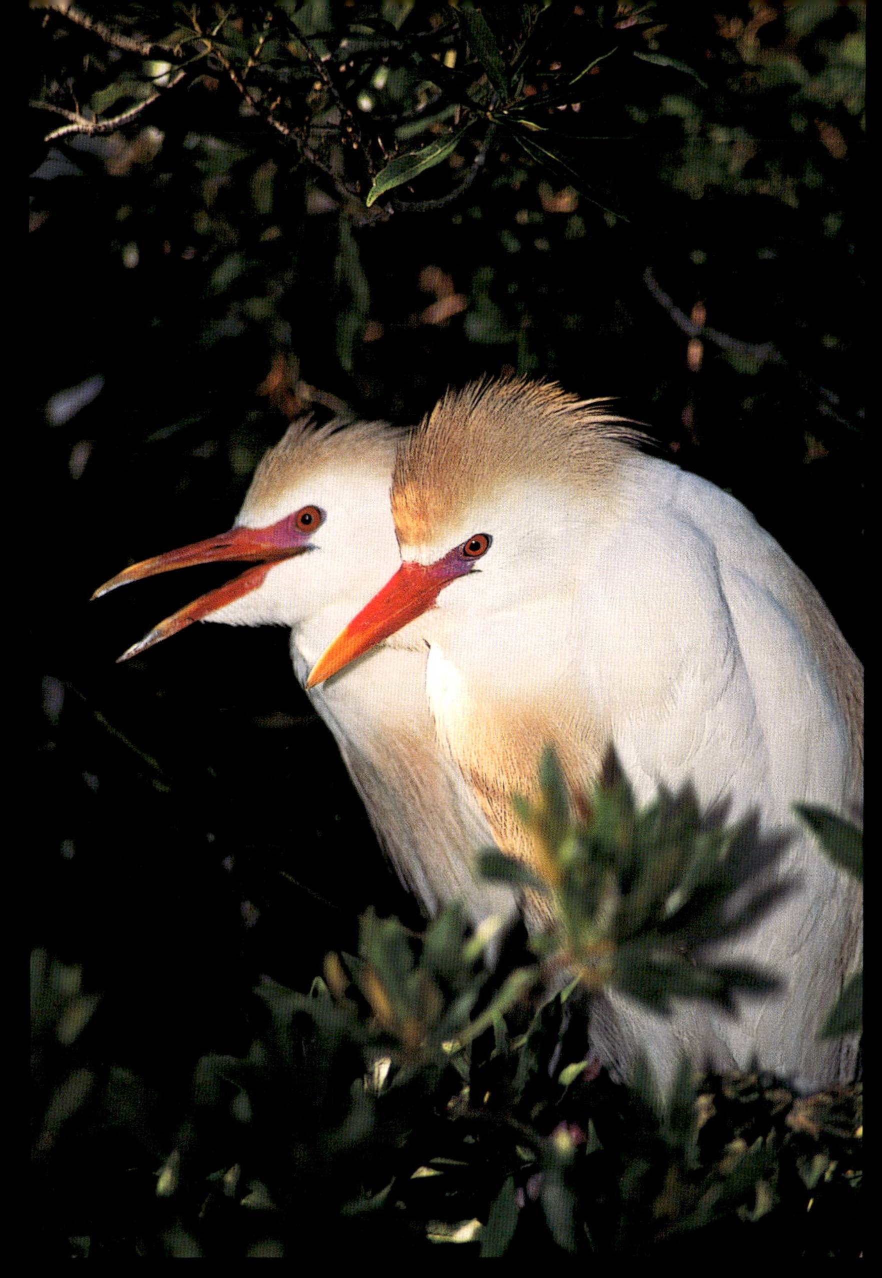

A flamboyant pair of cattle egrets in breeding plumage.

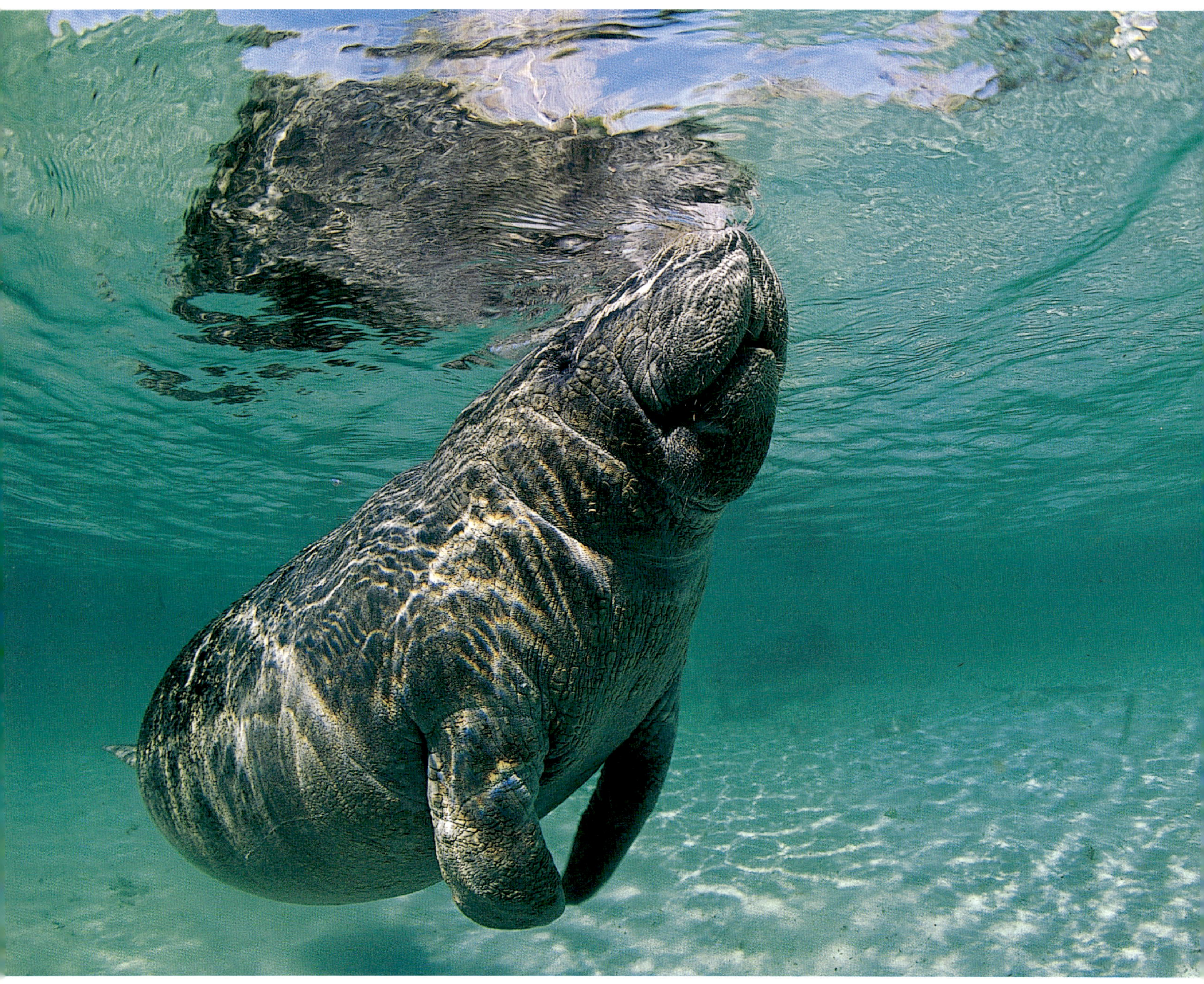

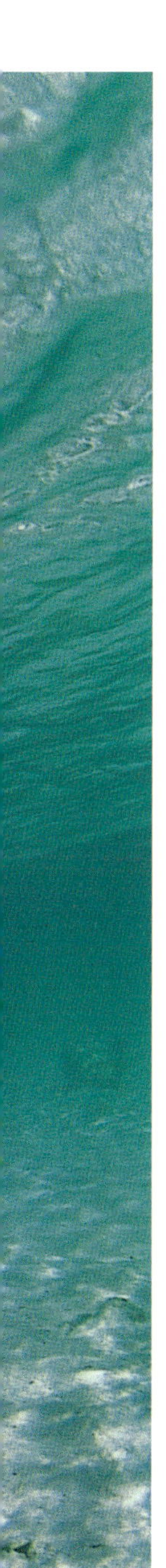

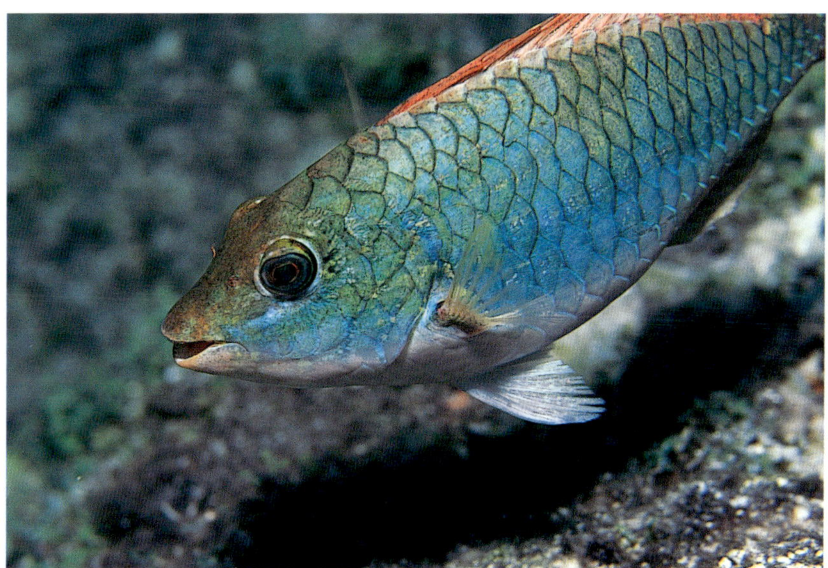

ABOVE: A juvenile redband parrotfish poses for the camera.

RIGHT: The spotted trunkfish is encased in an armor of plates instead of scales.

LEFT: A gentle manatee (or sea cow) surfaces for air at crystalline King's Bay, Crystal River.

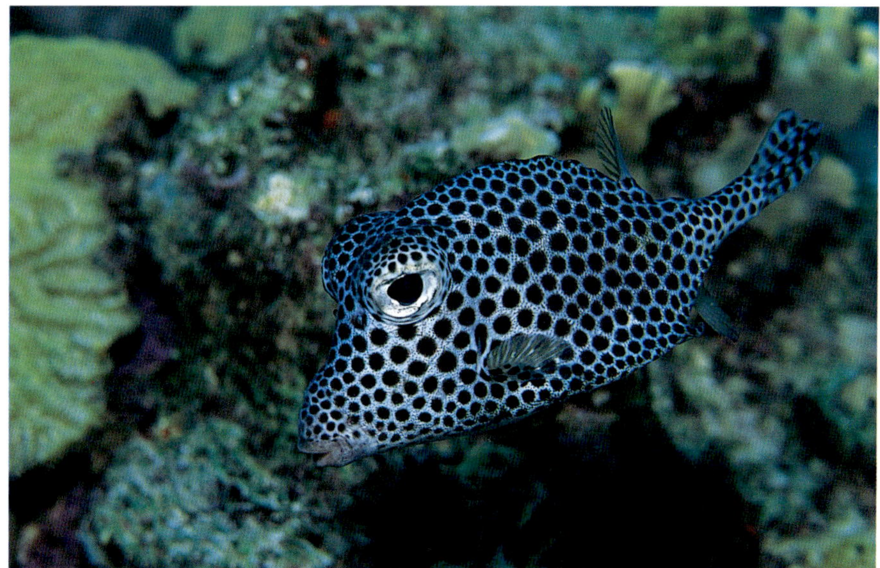

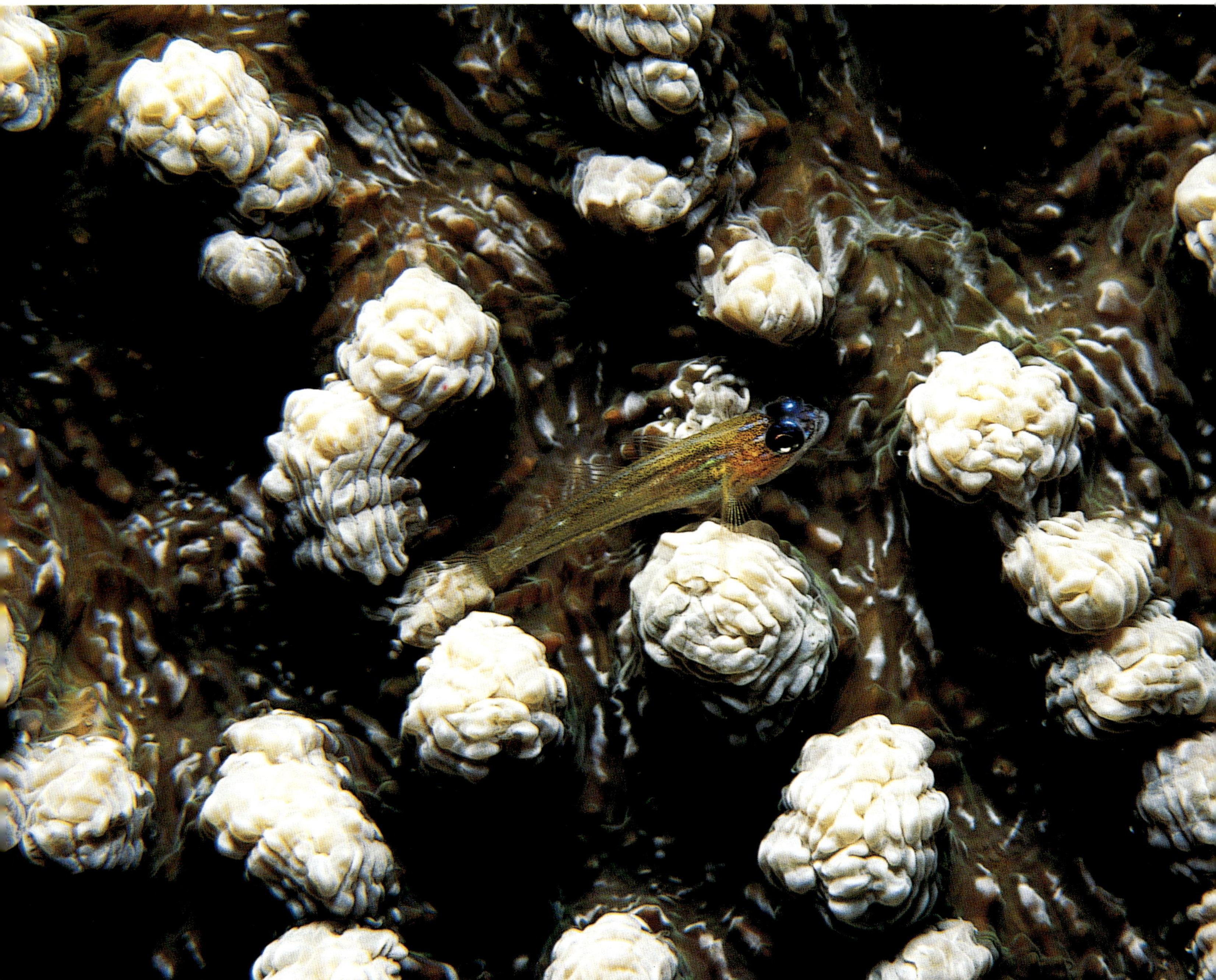

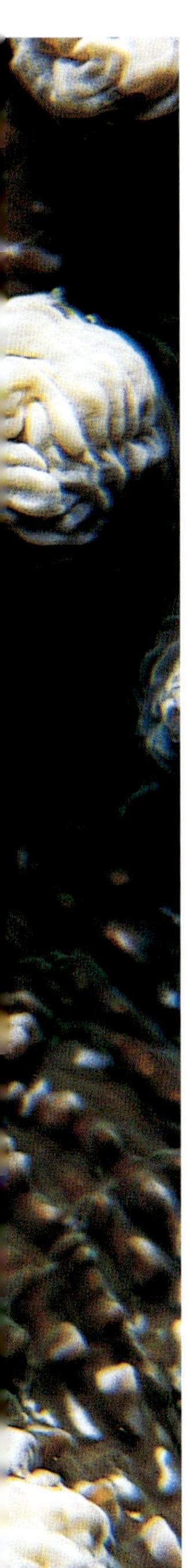

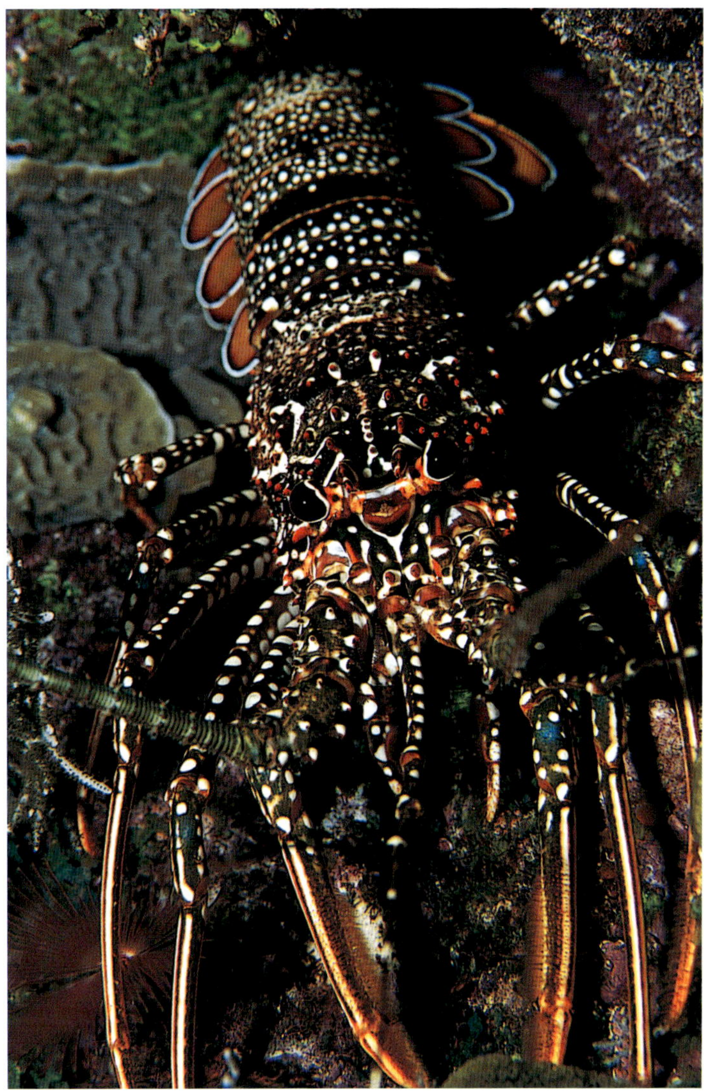

LEFT: A spotted lobster displays its vivid colors on a coral reef in the John Pennekamp Coral Reef State Park off Key Largo.

FAR LEFT: A diminutive peppermint goby nestles in the ridges of cactus coral.

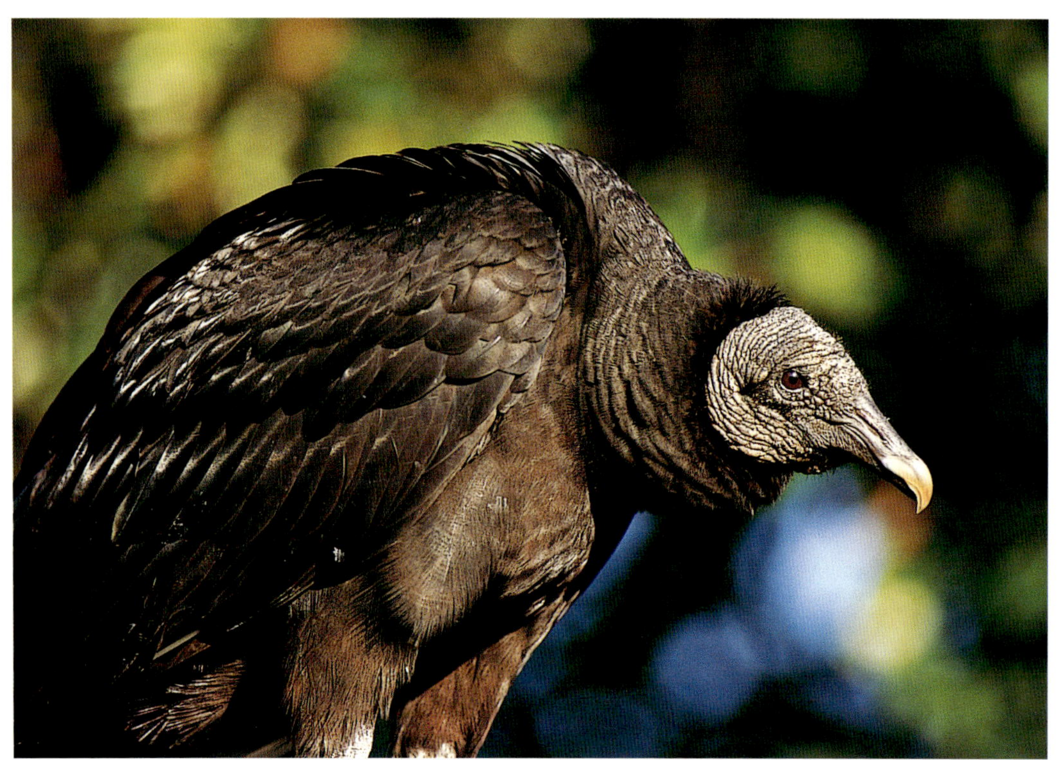

ABOVE: A black vulture waits for its next meal at the Royal Palm Visitor Center in Everglades National Park.

RIGHT: As its name indicates, the snail kite feeds mostly on snails. Pictured is a female. ERWIN & PEGGY BAUER/TOM STACK & ASSOCIATES

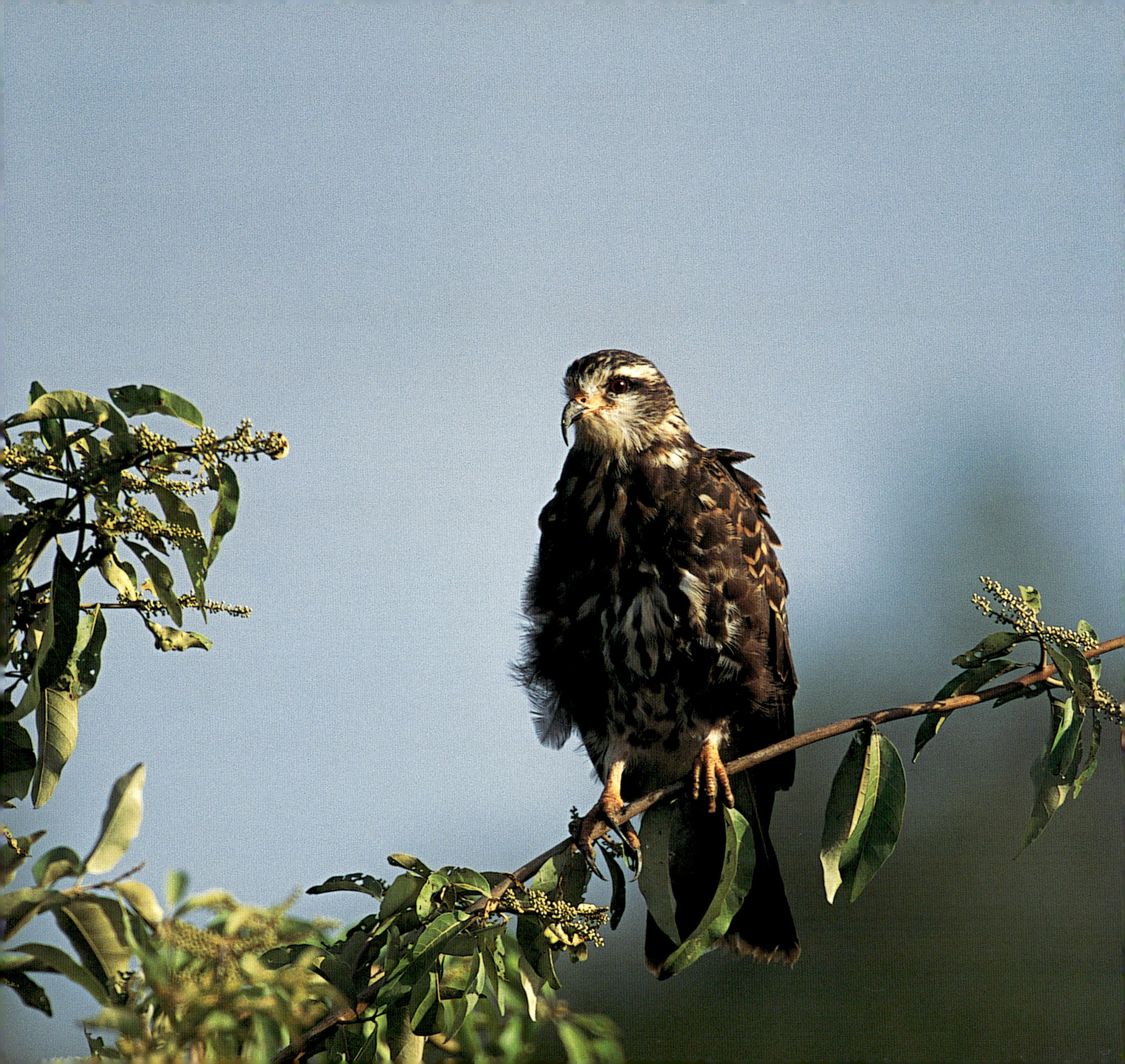

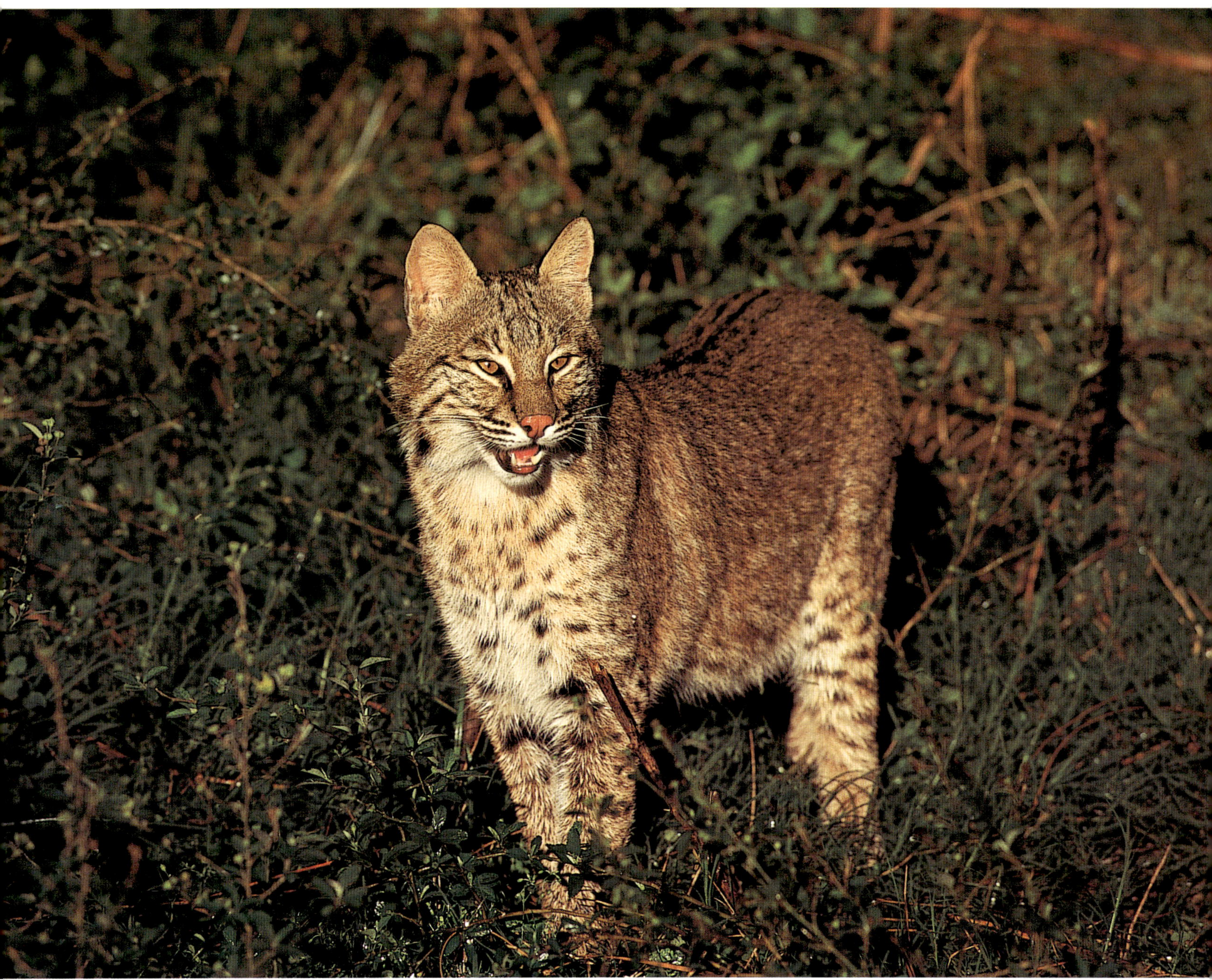

FACING PAGE: The Florida bobcat is darker in color than other bobcat subspecies. THOMAS KITCHIN/TOM STACK & ASSOCIATES

BELOW: While it may appear docile, the Florida softshell turtle has very powerful jaws and isn't shy about using them.

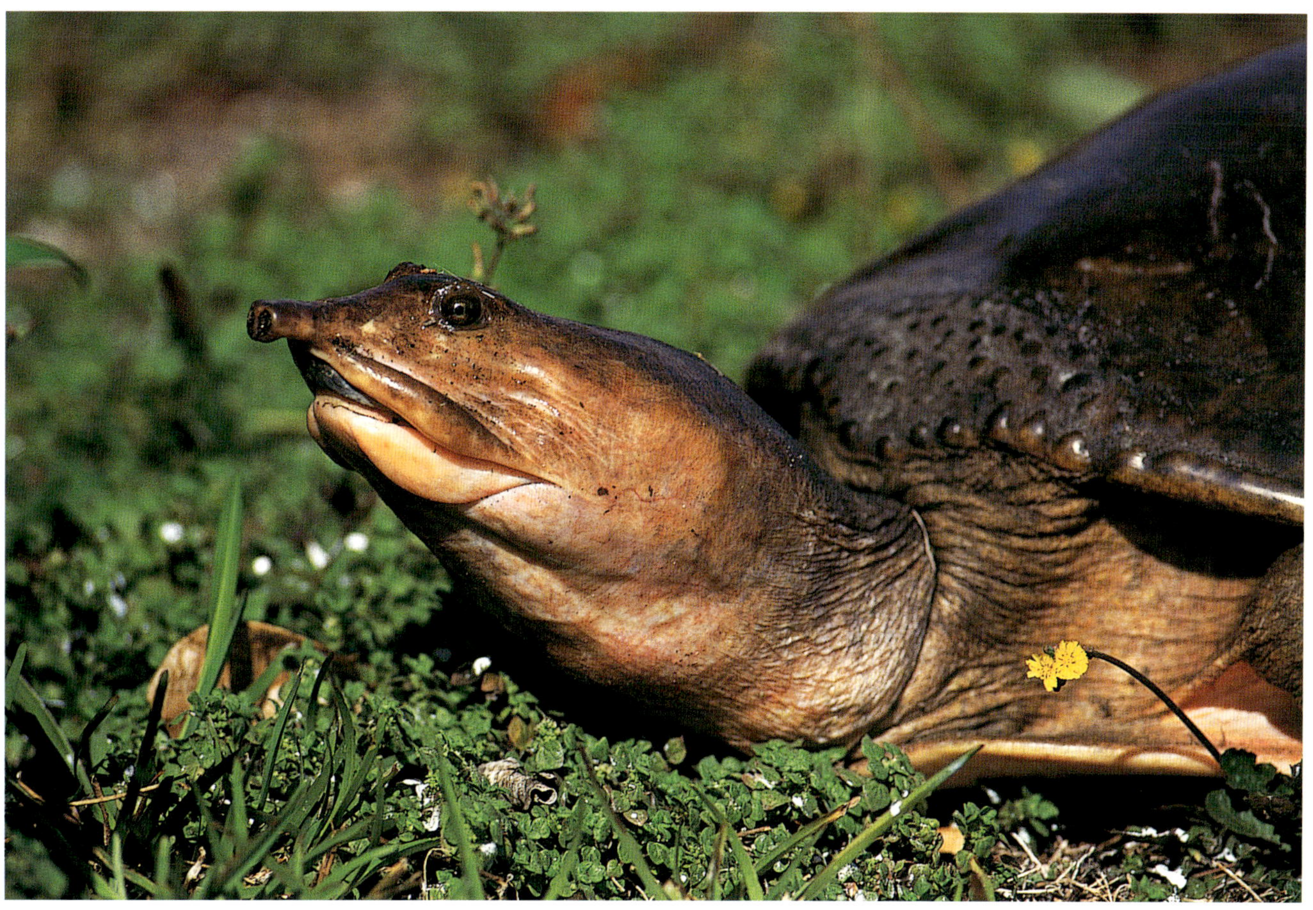

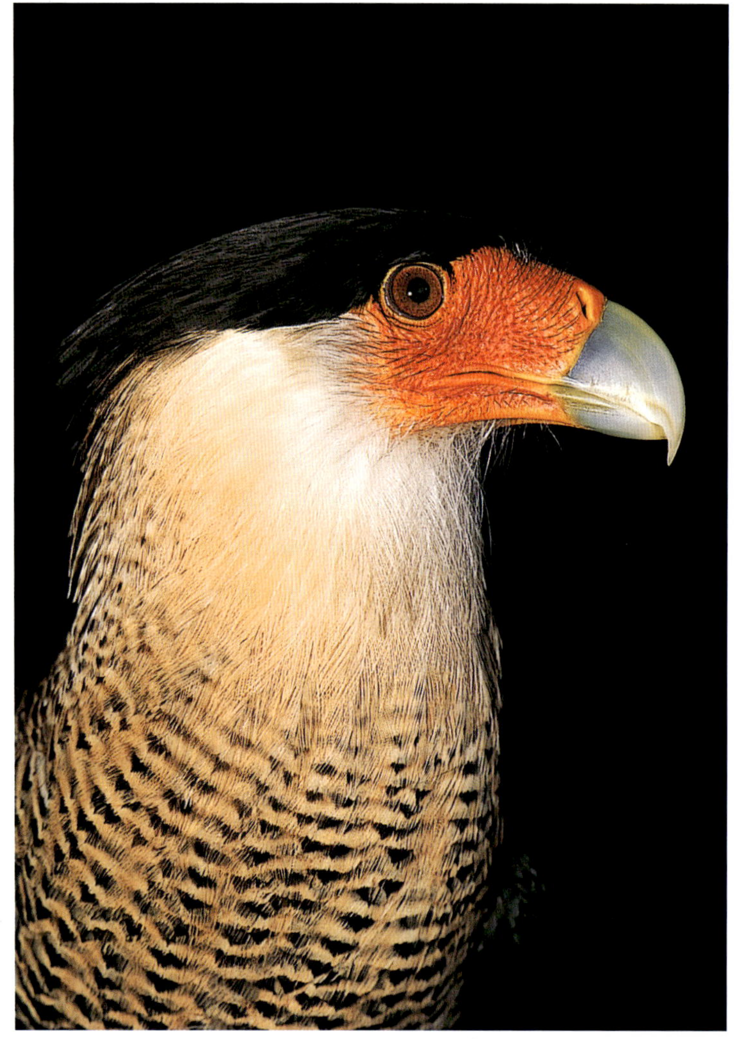

ABOVE: The crested caracara, a member of the falcon family, is one of Florida's most spectacular birds.

RIGHT: Typically an oceanic bird, the magnificent frigatebird roosts during the summer off both Florida coasts. Here a male inflates his throat pouch in a courtship display.

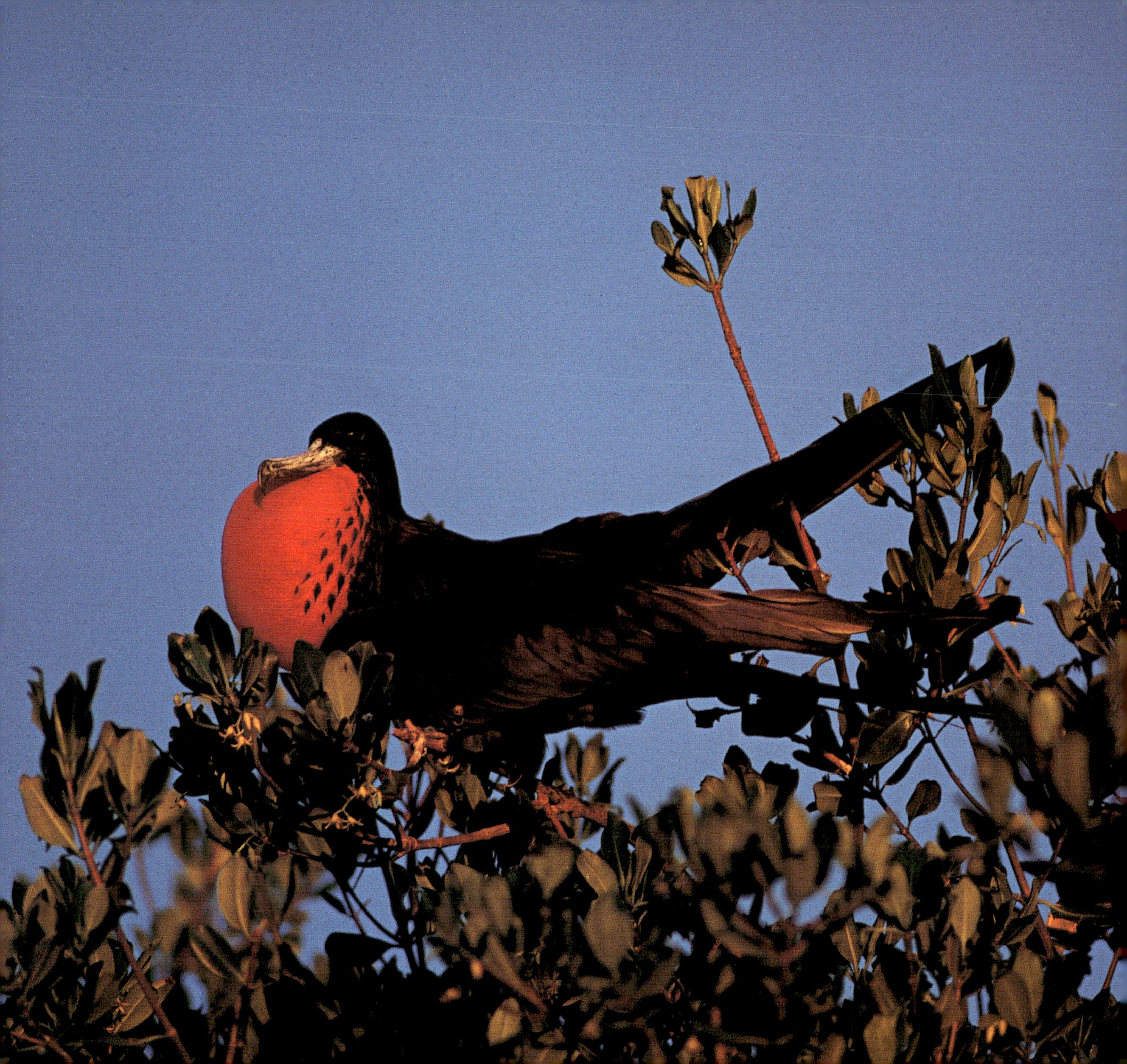

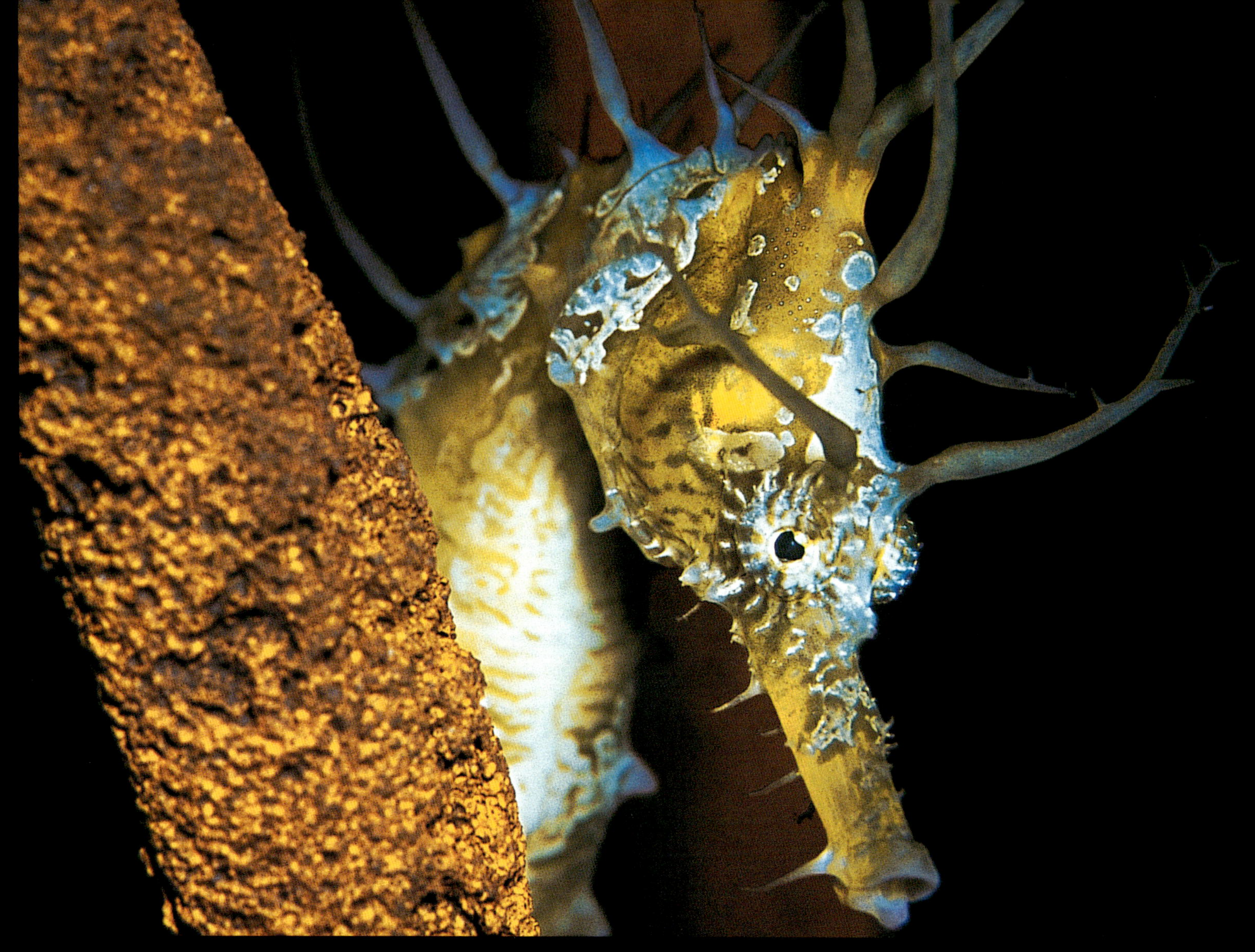

It is difficult to spot a camouflaged seahorse while snorkeling in shallow seagrass areas.

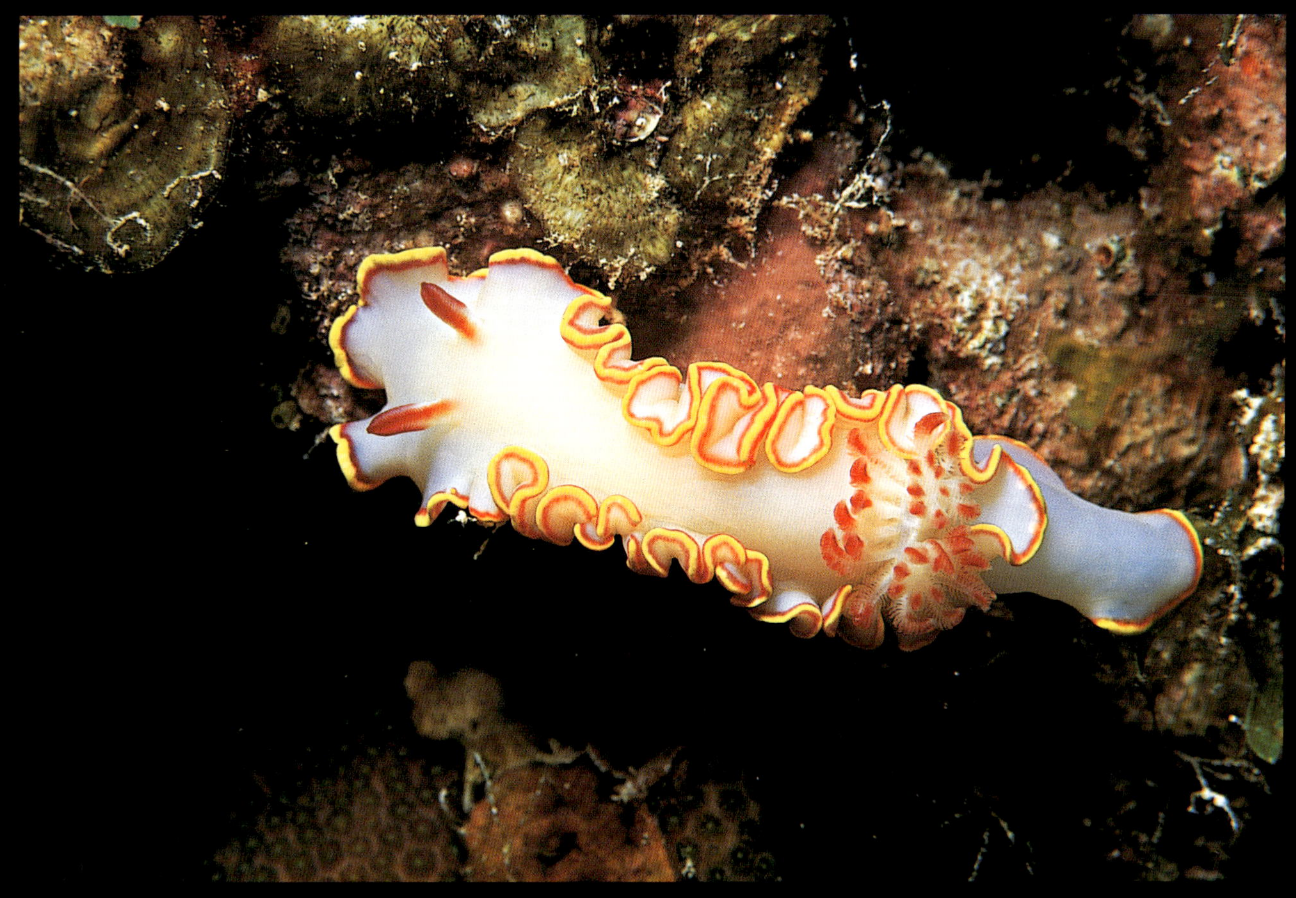

A two-inch-long, red-tipped sea goddess nudibranch adds a splash of color to Conch Reef off Tavernier.

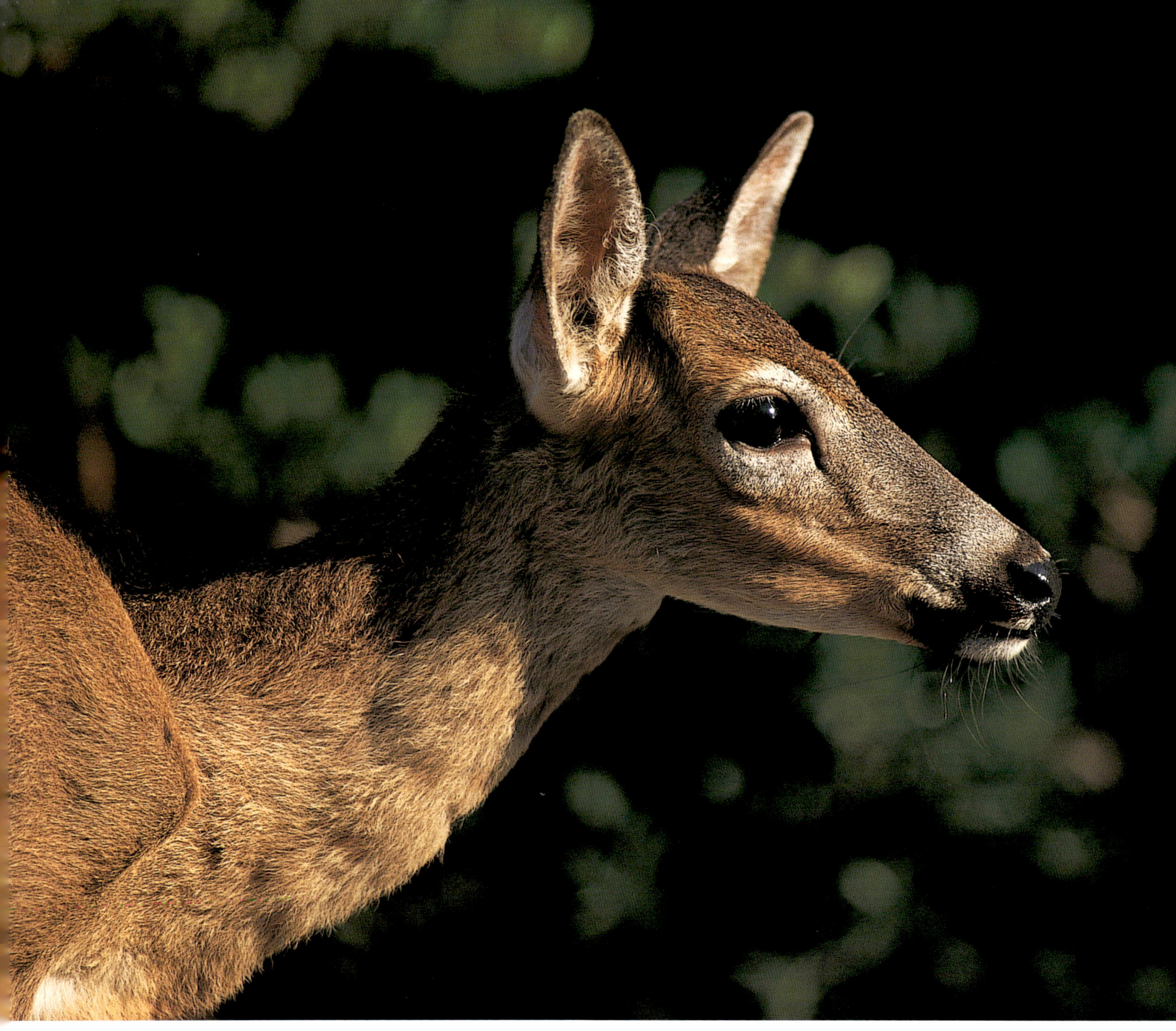

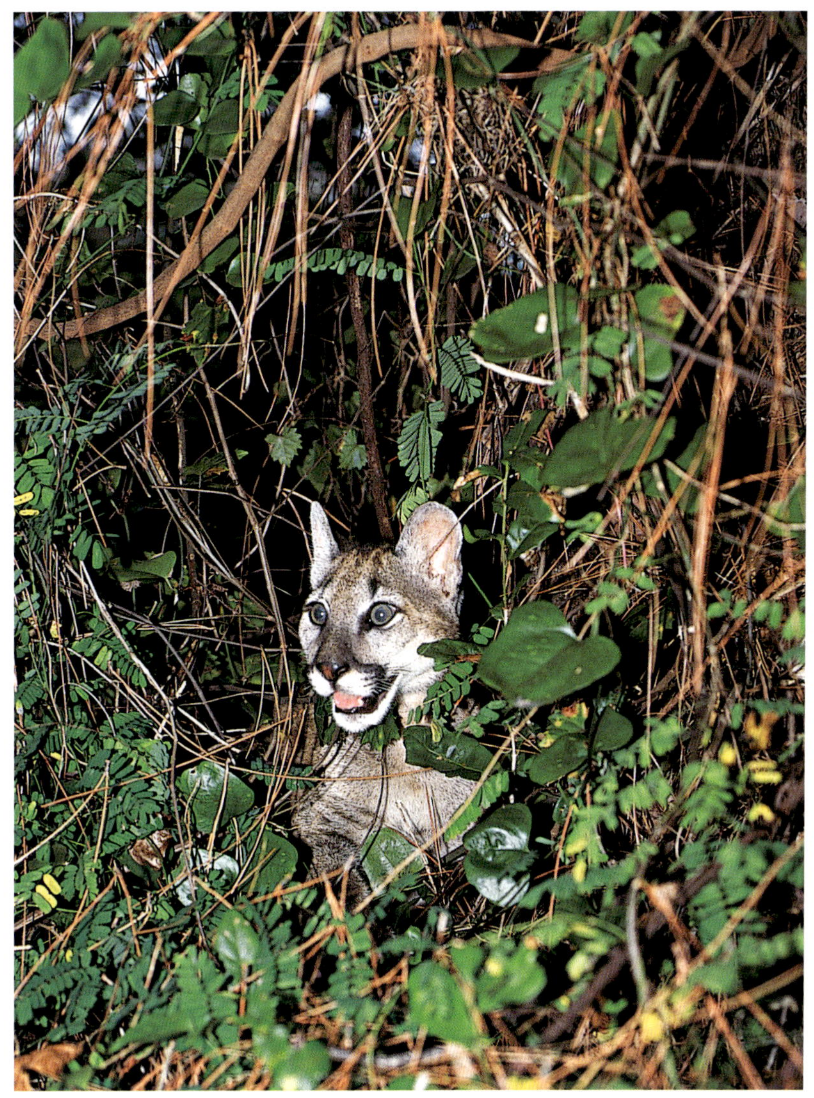

ABOVE: A Florida panther kitten gazes at the world outside its den.

LEFT: An alert key deer explores Big Pine Key.

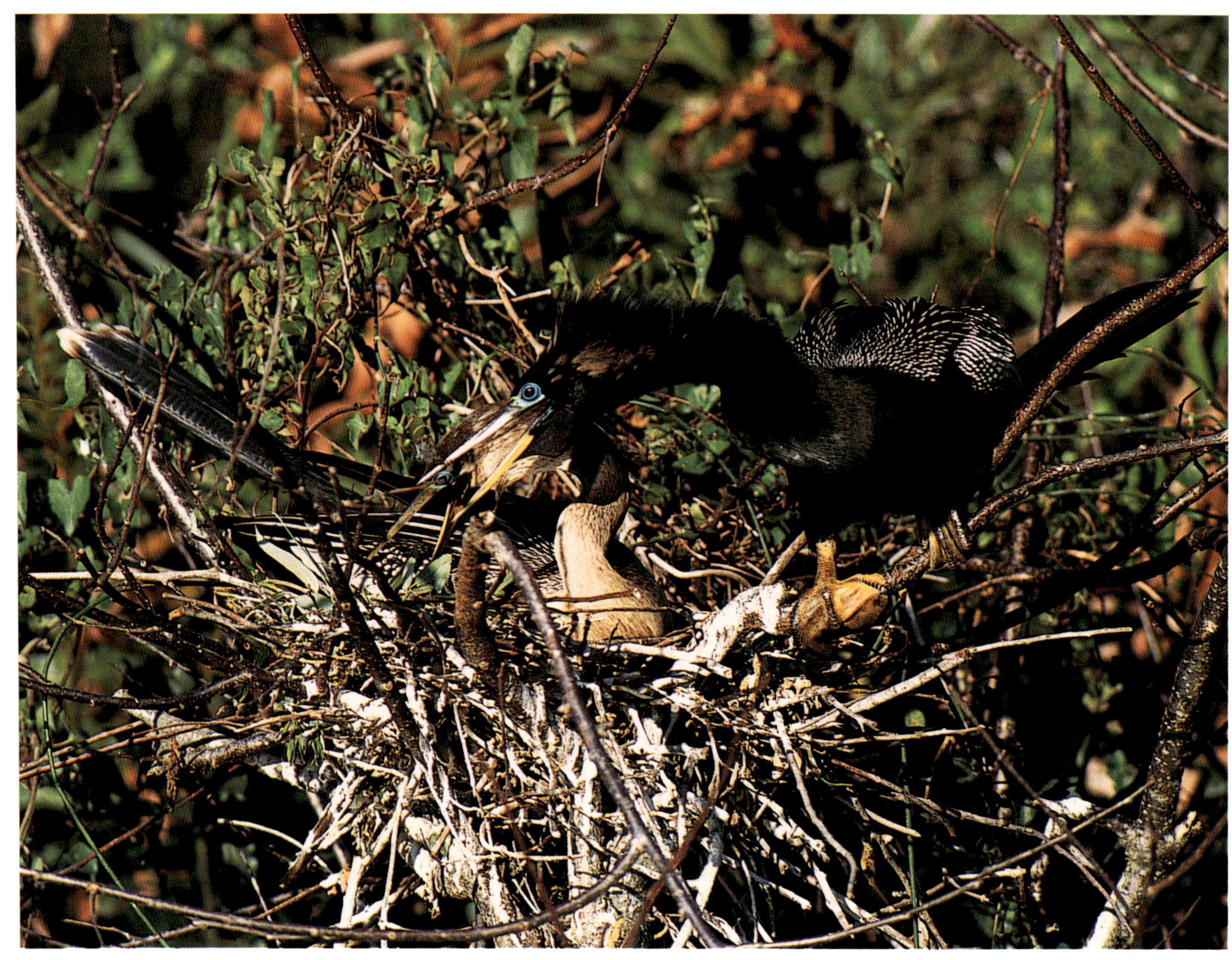

ABOVE: A mother anhinga attends to her young in the nest.

FACING PAGE: The limpkin, a freshwater wading bird, can be found throughout Florida. JEFF FOOTE/TOM STACK & ASSOCIATES

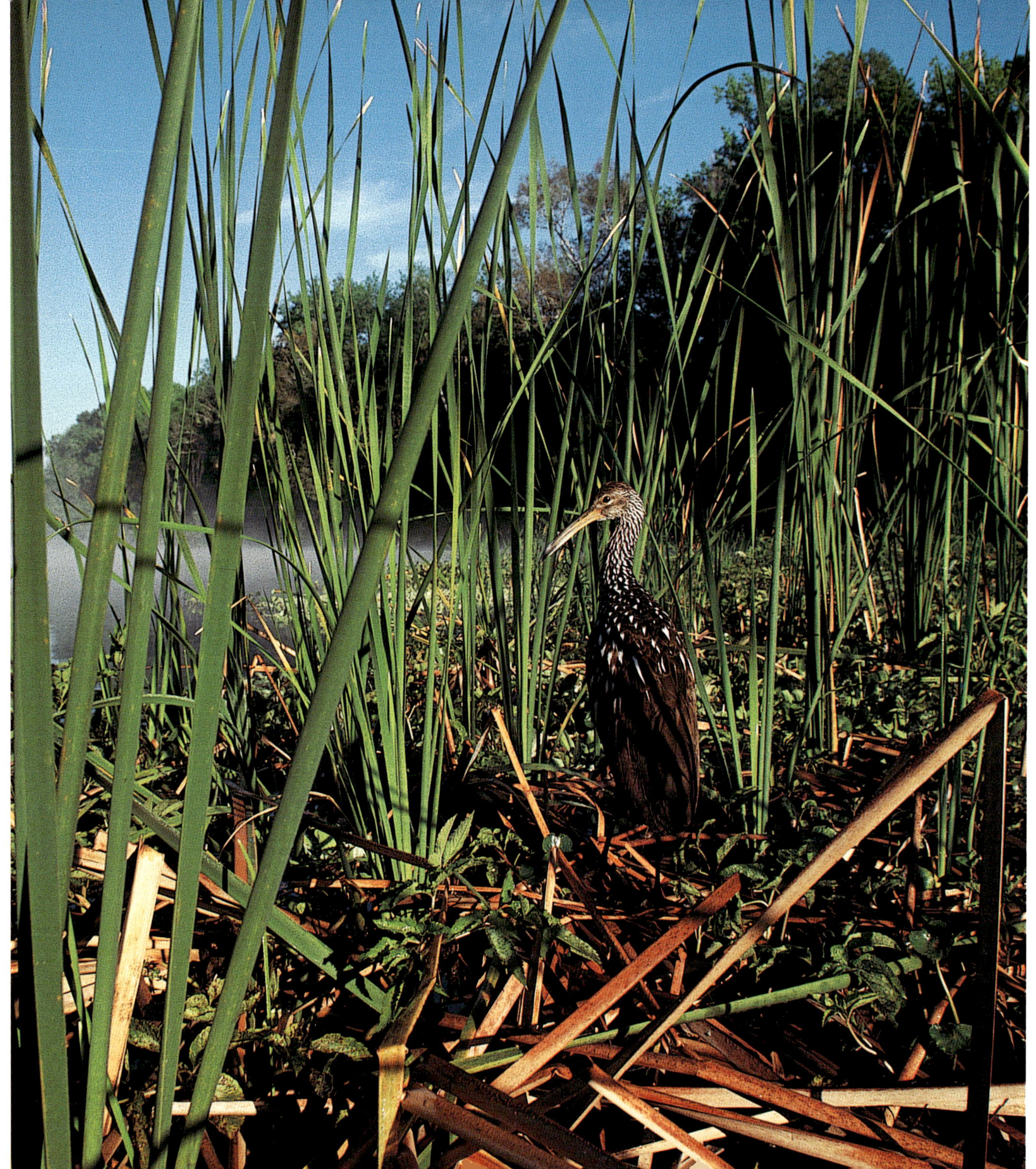

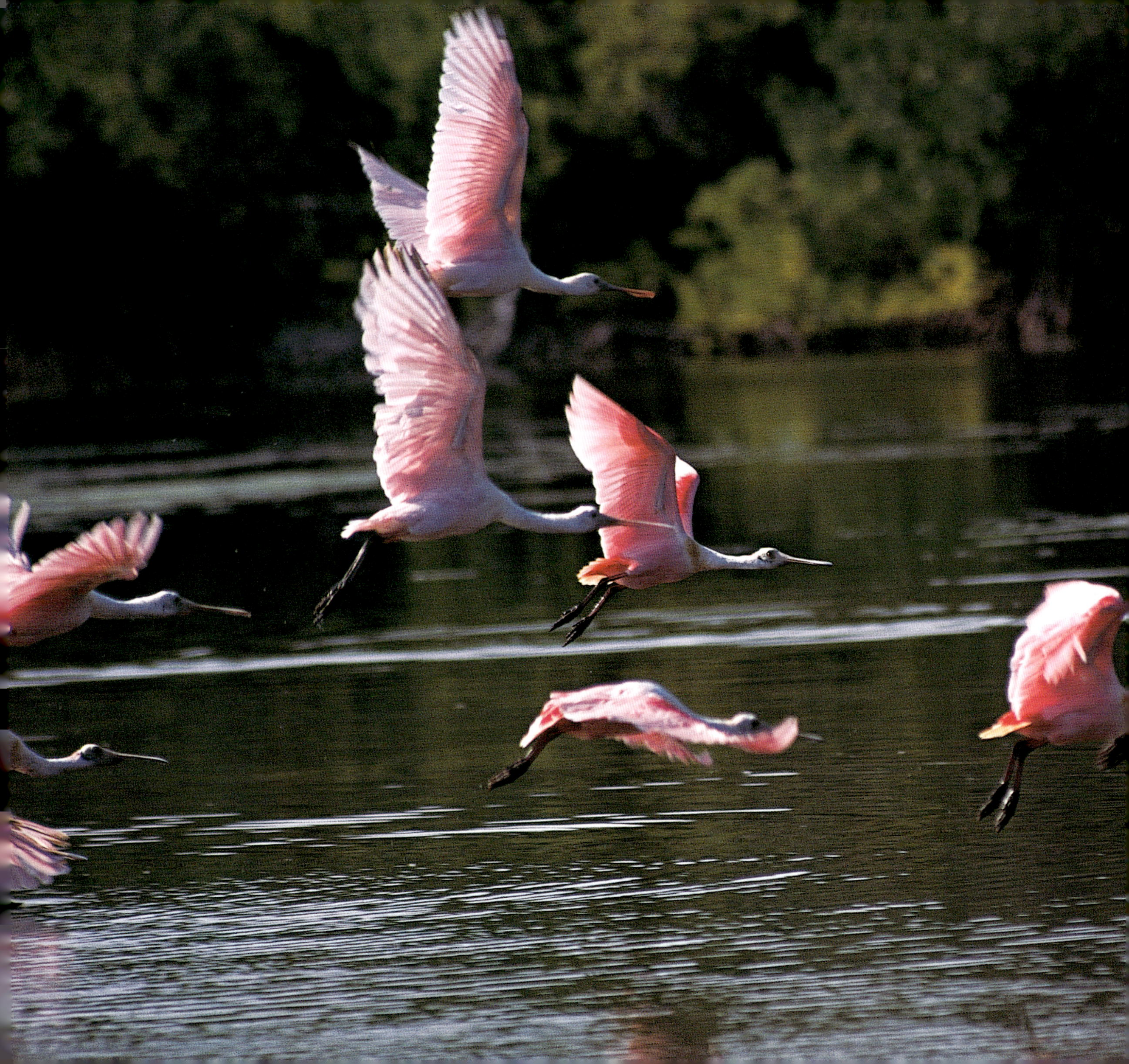

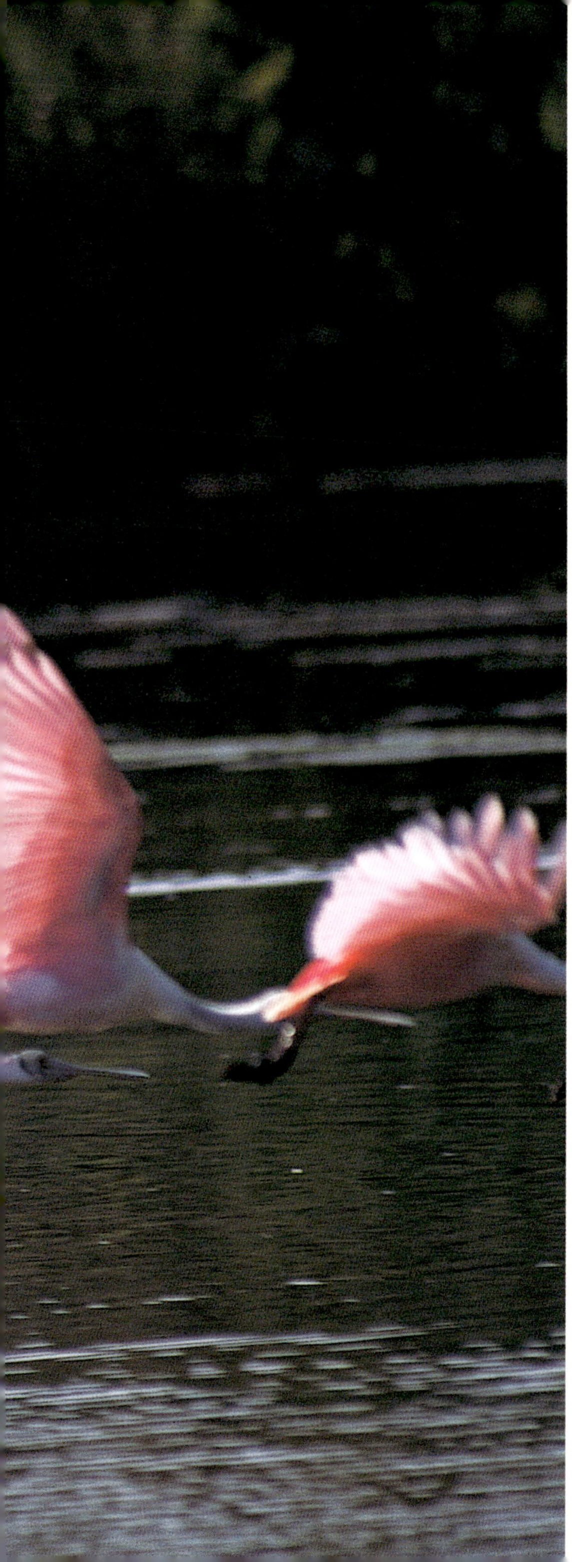

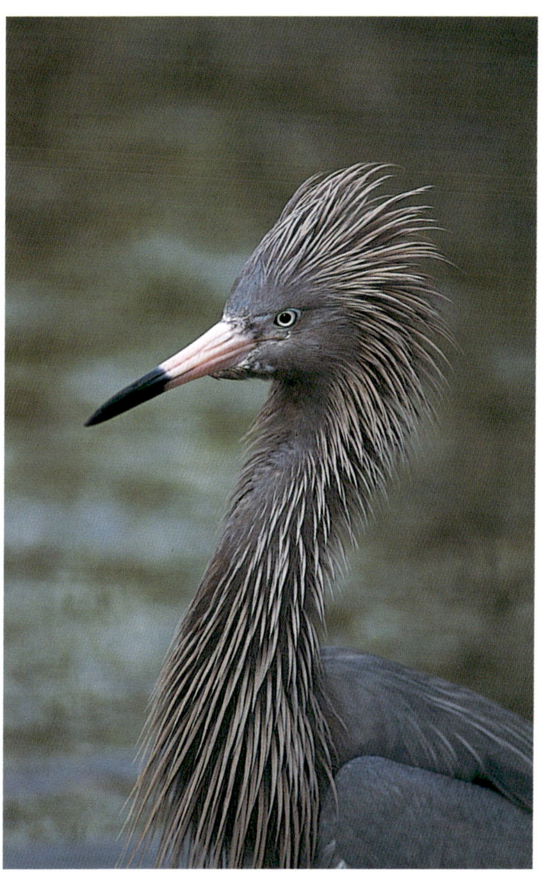

ABOVE: With its feathers ruffled, this reddish egret appears to be a bird with an attitude!

LEFT: A flock of roseate spoonbills takes to the air at J. N. "Ding" Darling National Wildlife Refuge on Sanibel Island.

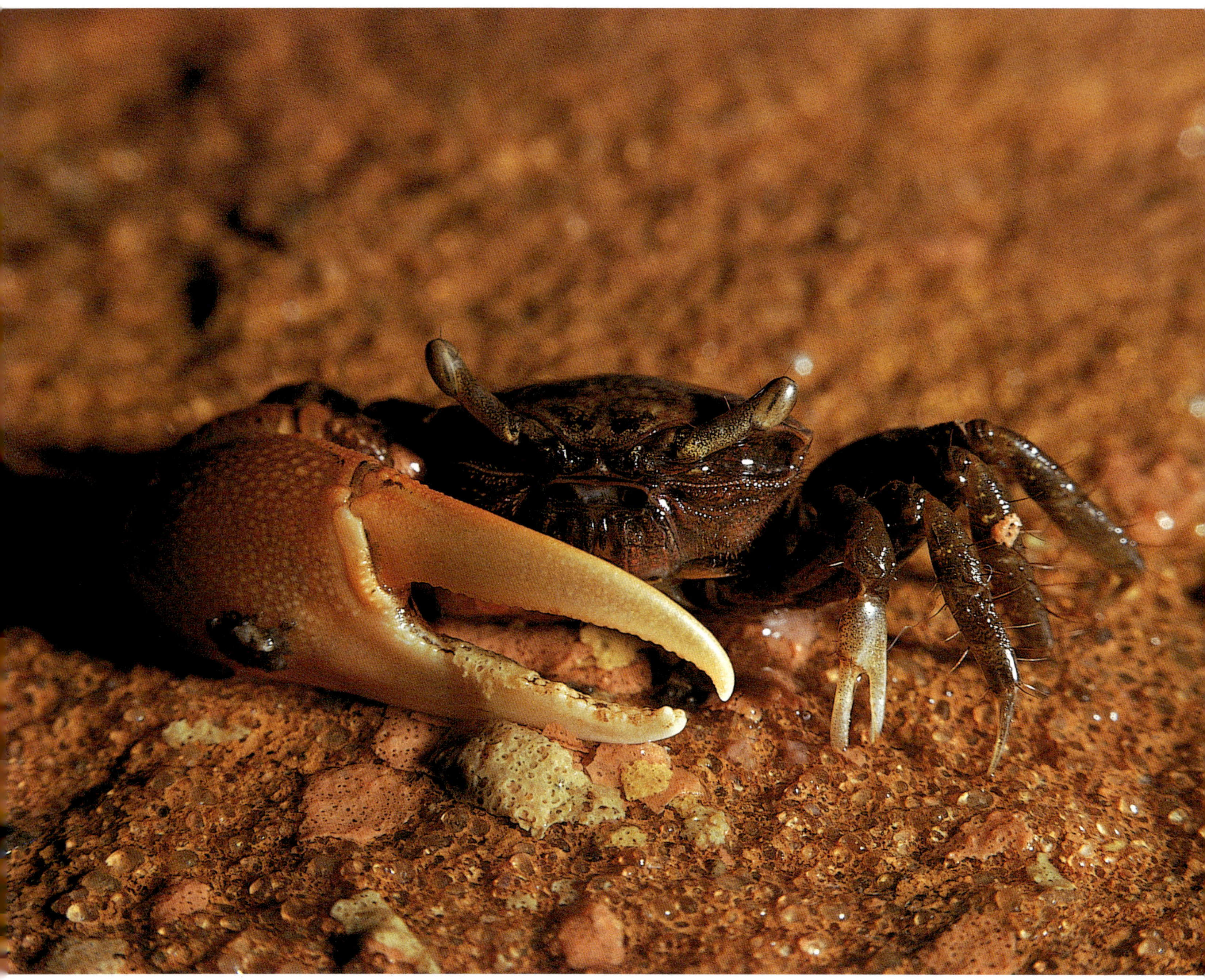

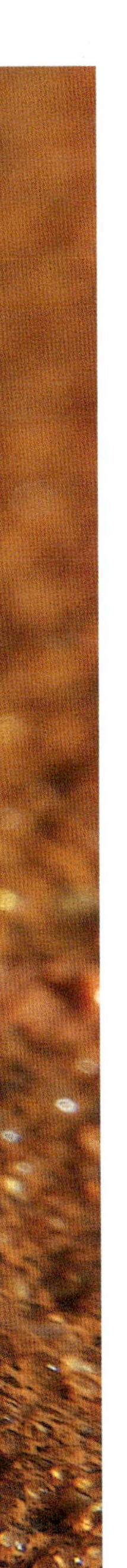

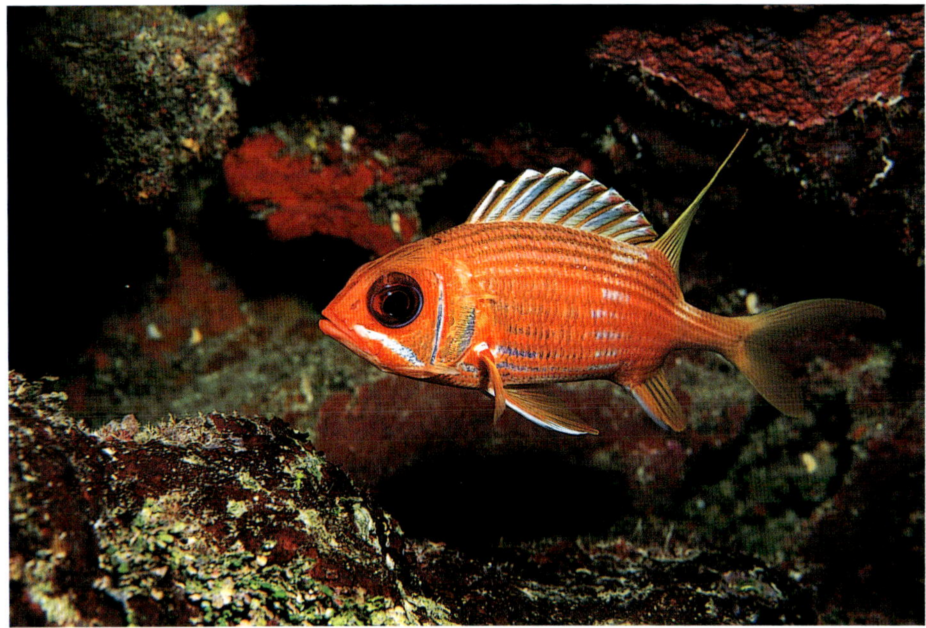

ABOVE: Nestled in a coral crevice, a longspine squirrel fish displays its dorsal fin off Key Largo.

RIGHT: The feeding tentacles of a feather duster worm filter microscopic plankton from the water.

LEFT: A male fiddler crab brandishes his large claw to attract females.

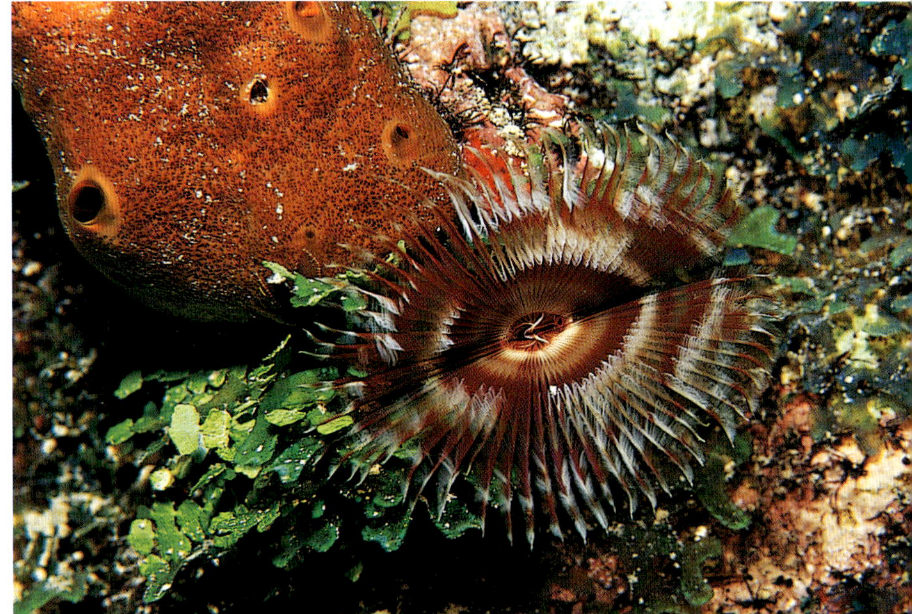

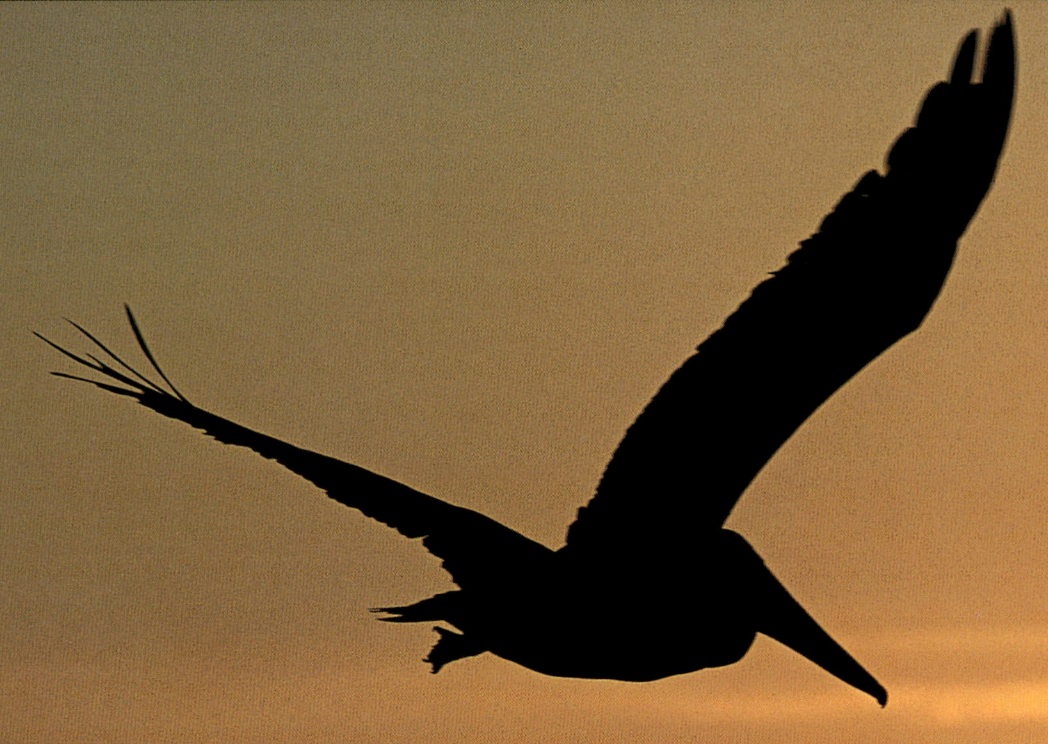

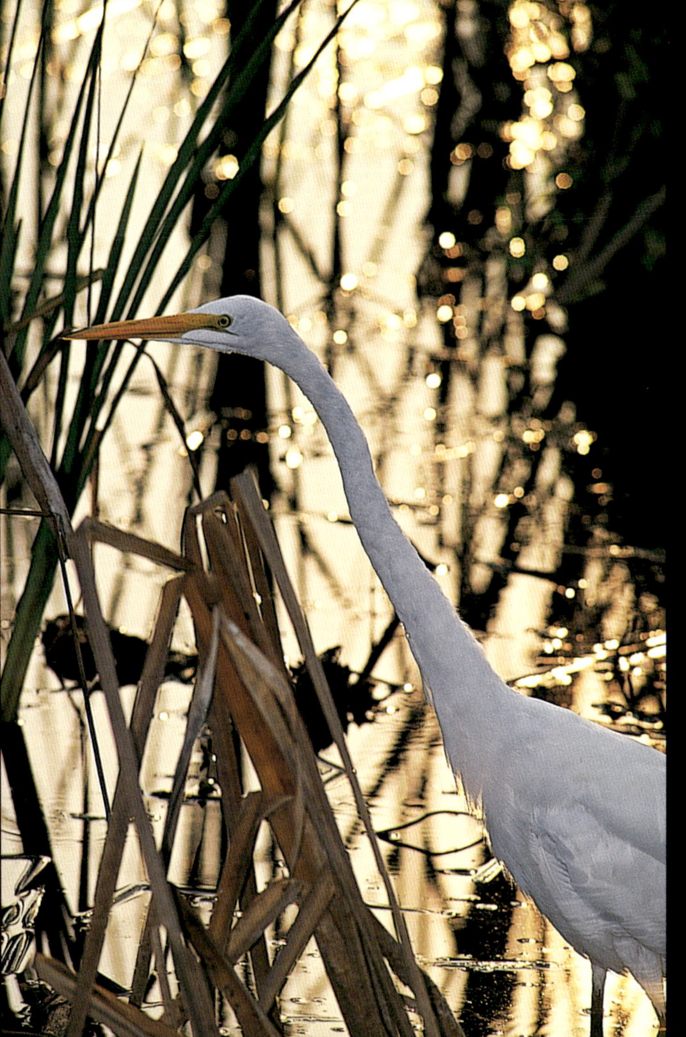

LEFT: An egret stalks dinner at Eco Pond in Everglades National Park.

FACING PAGE: Winging its way home, a brown pelican creates a striking silhouette at dusk.

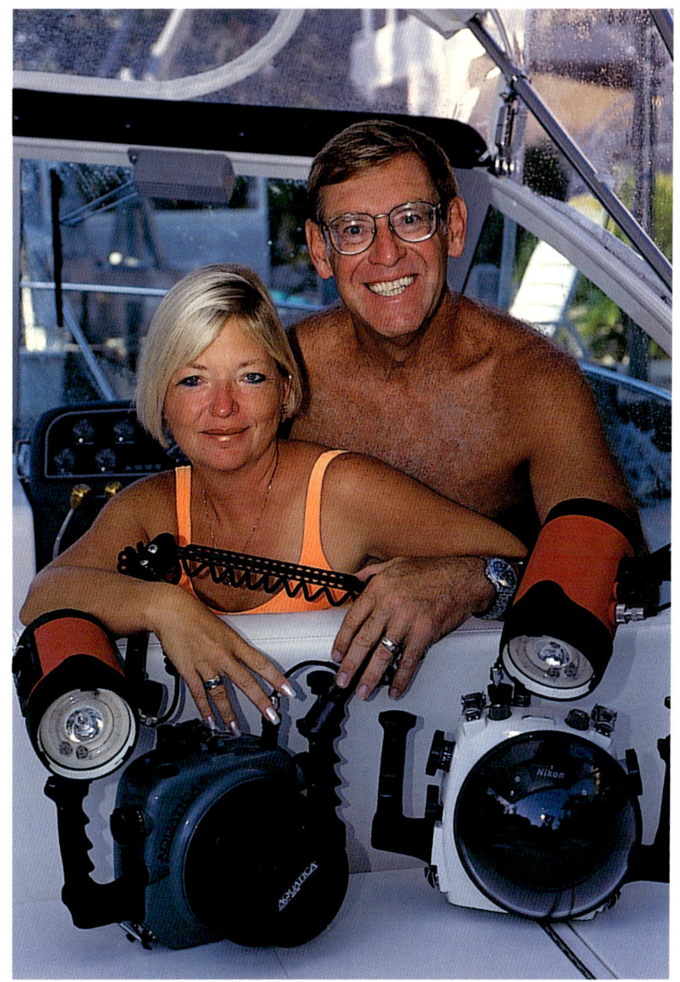

© MARK STACK

Respected as one of the world's most widely published photography couples, Tom and Therisa Stack are full-time professionals with more than thirty-five years of experience. From their home base in Key Largo, they journey on frequent assignments throughout the Florida Keys and Caribbean. They work closely with National Oceanic and Atmospheric Administration and Florida Keys National Marine Sanctuary researchers who are actively involved with the preservation of the fragile coral reef and mangrove ecosystems.

Their photography has been published in *National Geographic, National Wildlife, Audubon Magazine, Sierra Magazine, Travel & Leisure, Islands, Travel Holiday, Outside Magazine, Smithsonian Magazine, Backpacker, Nature Conservancy, National Parks, Blue Planet, Scuba Diving, Sport Diver, Geo, Canoe & Kayak Magazine, Yachting, Power & Motoryacht,* Discovery Channel Guides, Hallmark and American Greetings calendars, *Encyclopaedia Britannica, Encarta,* and many other books and magazines.

www.tomstackphoto.com